HEADLINE SERIES

No. 296   FOREIGN POLICY ASSOCIATION   Summer 1991

Political Tides in the Arab World

by Muhammad Muslih
and
Augustus Richard Norton

Introduction		3
1	**The Arab Crisis**	9
2	**Iraq's Invasion of Kuwait**	19
3	**Arab Systems of Government**	25
4	**New Political Alignments**	47
5	**Windows of Opportunity**	59
6	**Building on the Gulf Victory**	64
	Talking It Over	69
	Annotated Reading List	70

Cover Design: Ed Bohon $4.00
Photo: AP/Wide World Photos, Inc.

The Authors

MUHAMMAD MUSLIH is associate professor of political science and director of the International Relations Program at C.W. Post College, Long Island University. He holds a Ph.D. in political science from Columbia University and is the author of numerous works on Arab politics, including *From the Palestine War to the Gulf War: Palestinian Thought Since 1948* (forthcoming).

AUGUSTUS RICHARD NORTON is professor of political science at the United States Military Academy. He designed and directs (pro bono) a program on "Toward Enduring Peace in the Middle East" in cooperation with the International Peace Academy in New York City and with the support of the Ford and MacArthur foundations. His most recent articles on the Middle East have appeared in *Current History, Foreign Policy, The Middle East Journal* and leading newspapers.

The Foreign Policy Association

The Foreign Policy Association is a private, nonprofit, nonpartisan educational organization. Its purpose is to stimulate wider interest and more effective participation in, and greater understanding of, world affairs among American citizens. Among its activities is the continuous publication, dating from 1935, of the HEADLINE SERIES. The authors are responsible for factual accuracy and for the views expressed. FPA itself takes no position on issues of U.S. foreign policy.

HEADLINE SERIES (ISSN 0017-8780) is published four times a year, Winter, Spring, Summer and Fall, by the Foreign Policy Association, Inc., 729 Seventh Ave., New York, N.Y. 10019. Chairman, Michael H. Coles; President, R.T. Curran; Editor in Chief, Nancy L. Hoepli; Senior Editors, Ann R. Monjo and K.M. Rohan. Editorial intern, Melani Cammett. Subscription rates, $15.00 for 4 issues; $25.00 for 8 issues; $30.00 for 12 issues. Single copy price $4.00. Discount 25% on 10 to 99 copies; 30% on 100 to 499; 35% on 500 to 999; 40% on 1,000 or more. Payment must accompany all orders. Add $2.50 for postage. Second-class postage paid at New York, N.Y. POSTMASTER: Send address changes to HEADLINE SERIES, Foreign Policy Association, 729 Seventh Ave., New York, N.Y. 10019. Copyright 1992 by Foreign Policy Association, Inc. Design by K.M. Rohan. Printed at Science Press, Ephrata, Pennsylvania. Summer 1991. Published March 1992.

Library of Congress Catalog Card No. 91-078231
ISBN 0-87124-142-0

Introduction

The Persian Gulf crisis of 1990–91 has often been referred to as a watershed—one of those moments in history when profound changes, even a reconfiguration of political reality, occur. Some pundits were disappointed that sweeping changes did not occur instantly. Others have been overly hasty in declaring that the Middle East is returning to business as usual. This impatience—in an age of instant news when history plays out before our eyes—is explicable, but the history of the Middle East teaches us that the full impact of epochal change is felt over months and years, not hours and days. The consequences of earlier turning points in the modern Middle East—the breakup of the Ottoman Empire after World War I, the 1948 war between Israel and the Arab states, the 1956 Suez crisis, the Six-Day War in 1967, the October war of 1973 and the revolution in Iran—are still being felt today.

During World War I, Britain promised to grant independence to the Arabs in the Ottoman-controlled portions of Arab lands if the Arabs would revolt against the Turks, who were allied with Germany. The promise conflicted, however, with another British promise to agree to the establishment of a Jewish national home in Palestine. Whether or not Palestine was to be included in the areas to be accorded independence has been hotly debated ever since. Despite the British promises, following the war Britain and France proceeded to carve up the Ottoman Empire between themselves. Arab bitterness over secret agreements, in which Britain undertook to divide portions of the Middle East with other European powers, provided a focus for Arab nationalism in the ensuing years. Arab nationalist sentiments conflicted directly with Zionism, the ideology that expressed the desire of many Jews to establish a homeland in Palestine.

After World War II, the British withdrew from Palestine and left the future of the territory in the hands of the United Nations. In November 1947, the UN General Assembly passed a resolution partitioning Palestine into independent Arab and Jewish states, and internationalizing Jerusalem. The Arabs rejected the plan, fighting erupted, and Israel declared itself a sovereign state on May 14, 1948. An estimated 700,000 Palestinian Arabs became refugees, fleeing to the surrounding Arab countries, and especially to the Jordan river's West Bank, which had been seized by Jordan. The Palestinian exodus of 1948 was followed by an influx of 500,000 Jews from the Arab countries into Israel. Jerusalem, where the UN had called for the establishment of a permanent international regime, was instead claimed by Israel and Jordan and bisected by a no-man's-land. Thus, the 1948 war gave the world a new state, Israel, and created a new diaspora, the scattering of the Palestinian Arabs.

The 1948 war also had a decisive impact within Egypt, where the incompetence of King Farouk's army against the forces of the nascent Israeli state helped to embolden the young officers who overthrew the monarch in 1952. The leader of the young officers was Gamal Abdel Nasser, who was to become the dominant political leader of the 1950s and 1960s—until his death in 1970.

In 1956, Britain and France, in collaboration with Israel, attacked Egypt in an attempt to seize the Suez Canal and topple Nasser, who had nationalized the canal. Under heavy pressure from the United States (and unvarnished threats from the Soviet Union), the attackers were forced to back down without achieving their war aims. In the process, Nasser acquired a reputation as a great Arab hero and the very symbol of Arab nationalism (the ideology that espoused the concept of the Arabs constituting a single nation, one that had been fragmented as a result of imperialism).

The Suez crisis heralded the decline of British and French influence in the Middle East, and the emergence of the great cold-war rivalry in the region between the United States and the Soviet Union.

In 1957 Arab nationalist officers in the Jordanian army tried unsuccessfully to overthrow King Hussein. In February 1958 Egypt and Syria formed the United Arab Republic, a union which lasted a little over three years. Also in 1958, the pro-British monarchy in Iraq was overthrown, and a civil war between pro-Nasser and anti-Nasser forces broke out in Lebanon. The French government had calculated that if it defeated Nasser at Suez, it would cut off a main source of outside support for the Algerian rebels and preserve the colony as an integral part of France. Instead, the French Fourth Republic itself fell in 1958, and France barely averted an insurrection within its own military. Algeria won its independence in 1962.

The Six-Day War

In 1967, a time of mounting tension between Israel and its Arab neighbors, Israel launched the June war, responding to provocations by its Arab enemies, and dealt a crippling blow to the air forces of Egypt, Jordan and Syria. Militarily the Six-Day War was a stunning success for Israel. By the war's end, Israel had tripled the territory under its control by taking the Gaza Strip and the Sinai Peninsula from Egypt, the West Bank and East Jerusalem from Jordan, and the Golan Heights from Syria. Until 1967, the Palestinians had put their faith in the Arab governments, but the Six-Day War changed all that. The war gave new credibility to the Palestinian guerrilla organizations, which spread a message of popular revolution. The Palestinian groups grew rapidly, seizing every opportunity—from hijacking airplanes to organizing protests—to publicize their Palestinian nationalist demands. The radical Palestinian groups waged a violent campaign. In the resulting spiral of attack and counterattack, innocents often paid the costs for vengeance. In September 1970 civil war broke out in Jordan between armed Palestinians and the Jordanian army after a series

of increasingly blatant challenges by the Palestine Liberation Organization (PLO) to the Jordanian regime. The Palestinians were defeated decisively and fled to Lebanon where they established new armed bases under the loose control of the PLO. The introduction of the armed Palestinian presence undermined Lebanon's fragile stability and contributed to the outbreak of civil war in 1975. The war erupted with full force in 1976 with the PLO as one of the major combatants.

By the autumn of 1973 Israel was consolidating its control over the lands it had seized in the 1967 war. In Egypt, Anwar al-Sadat had assumed the presidency following Nasser's death in September 1970. Initially, and it turned out, incorrectly, Sadat was widely dismissed as a political lightweight more notable for his blustery rhetoric and empty promises of action against Israel than as a shrewd geopolitician. Even when he moved decisively his actions seemed rash and poorly calculated. For instance, in 1972 he expelled all of the Soviet Union's military advisers from Egypt, prompting an incredulous Henry Kissinger, then national security adviser to President Richard M. Nixon, to note that Sadat had failed to exact a price for his action from Washington. The expulsion decree was simply a welcome gift with no recompense promised, solicited or offered.

Camp David Accords

But the underrated Sadat, in collusion with Syria's President Hafez al-Assad, launched a surprise campaign against Israel in October 1973 and thereby set in train a series of diplomatic achievements which ended with the Camp David accords in 1978 and the 1979 peace treaty between Israel and Egypt. In the course of the war, the world discovered a new global-power factor, oil, as the Arab oil producers invoked an embargo which created gas lines in the United States and Europe and marked the end of cheap oil. The war propelled Saudi Arabia, with its vast oil wealth, to a position of unforeseen power and influence on the world scene.

No doubt, the October war was the mechanism through which Egypt recovered the Sinai Peninsula and escaped from the economic trap of the Arab-Israeli conflict, but Egypt's peace with Israel freed the Jewish state for a grandiose misadventure in Lebanon. With Egypt's military power truncated from any Arab military coalition, Israel's Defense Minister Ariel Sharon could now turn his attention northward to Lebanon where he saw an opportunity to defeat the PLO, extricate Syria from the country and reach a second peace treaty with a friendly and pliant government in Beirut, the Lebanese capital. Sharon miscalculated though, and the Israeli invasion instead produced a significant defeat of Israeli military power, at unlikely hands. The Lebanese resistance fighters, many of them Shiite militiamen who had taken up arms against the PLO before 1982, were outgunned and vastly outnumbered by the Israeli army, but they forced an Israeli withdrawal from most of Lebanon by 1985. The example of the resistance in Lebanon became a decisive inspiration for the Palestinians in the West Bank and Gaza, where the *intifada* (uprising) burst on the scene in late 1987.

Before Mohammad Reza Shah Pahlavi was forced to flee in 1979, non-Arab Iran was a pillar of American security strategy in the Middle East, particularly in the Persian Gulf. The self-styled Islamic revolution of Ayatollah Ruhollah Khomeini was an earthquake, shaking U.S. policy assumptions to their core and sending tremors throughout the Arab and Muslim worlds, from Morocco to Indonesia. In the Gulf states, in Lebanon and elsewhere, formerly quiescent communities of Shiite Muslims took inspiration from the success of Iran's Shiites. The Shiites, who only account for about 10 percent of all Muslims, have been victimized by centuries of discrimination in the Arab lands, and are, in effect, a political and economic underclass.

In an attempt to capitalize on what he perceived to be a moment of profound Iranian weakness, Iraq's President Saddam Hussein invaded Iran in 1980. By launching what would become a costly war for both Iran and Iraq, the Iraqi president gave early evidence of his capacity for miscalculation. The Iraqi leader assumed that Iran, wracked by revolution, would be easily and quickly defeated. Instead, Iran proved to be a stubborn adversary, and the Iran-Iraq War lasted for eight gruesome years.

Saddam Hussein's first war enjoyed the support of many Arab and even Western governments, who were apprehensive that the revolutionary forces unleashed in Iran would cause havoc unless they were checked. One by-product of the Iran-Iraq War was the Iran-contra affair, in which the United States, in a series of secret deals, sold Iran weapons with which to fight Iraq in order to win the freedom of Western hostages being held in Lebanon.

All of these earlier turning points illustrate the predictable unpredictability of political developments in the Middle East. They also show their far-reaching consequences.

Even by Middle East standards, the recent events in the Gulf promise to be of momentous importance. Although relatively few Arabs are still animated by the unification dreams of the late President Nasser, most Arabs share the belief that they are part of a single Arab nation. Thus, when Iraq invaded another Arab state, Kuwait, it struck a blow at the core of Arab identity and exposed the underlying divisions in the Arab world. Those divisions separate the rich from the poor and the privileged from the humble.

One palpable result of the Gulf crisis is that it exposed what many Arab intellectuals and some policymakers have called a malaise that afflicts Arab society and politics. Two manifestations of this malaise are the absence of democracy and the uneven distribution of wealth and population in the Arab world. Although his drive for self-aggrandizement, his obsession with foreign conspiracies, and his country's economic and territorial claims all played a role, Saddam Hussein could not have blundered into the suicidal venture in Kuwait if there been a minimum level of genuine political consultation in Iraq.

Western policymakers seem reluctant to articulate a vision for achieving political freedom in the Arab world because, in the short run, loosening the grip of authoritarian regimes could be a messy process. But statesmen with a longer view of history will understand that promoting the liberalization of Arab politics is the antidote to absolute rulers like Saddam Hussein.

Acknowledgment

Some of the ideas elaborated on here first appeared in the authors' "The Need for Arab Democracy," Foreign Policy, *Summer, 1991. A small portion of material on the UN in the Gulf crisis appears in Norton's chapter in Ibrahim Ibrahim, ed.,* The Gulf Crisis: Background and Consequences *(Washington, D.C., Georgetown University Center for Contemporary Arab Studies, 1992) and is used here with permission. Some material from Norton's "Breaking through the Wall of Fear in the Arab World," in* Current History, *January 1992, is used here with permission.*

The Arab Crisis

The Arab world presents a mixed picture of wealth and poverty, stability and instability, progress and stagnation. Today there are 21 Arab League member states with a total population of some 200 million people. Although the Arabs do not constitute a single nation-state in the Western sense of the word, they all cherish the Arabic language and a rich and glorious cultural heritage. In parts of the Arab world there is an abundance of natural resources, especially oil and minerals, though not foodstuffs. Economically speaking, the performance of the Arabs over the past 45 years has been adequate in some countries and impressive in others, as is evidenced by the increase in per capita gross national product (GNP), urbanization, mechanization, and other indices of modernization. In the field of education, Arab performance has also been good to very good, with some Arab states achieving high levels of literacy. In the political and intellectual realms, however, the picture is different. Indeed in many respects it is bleak.

The political changes that have engulfed the world in recent years have hardly touched most Arab states. Rulers with unchecked powers continue to reign supreme. The gap between the haves and the have-nots is ever widening. Fragmentation persists, and

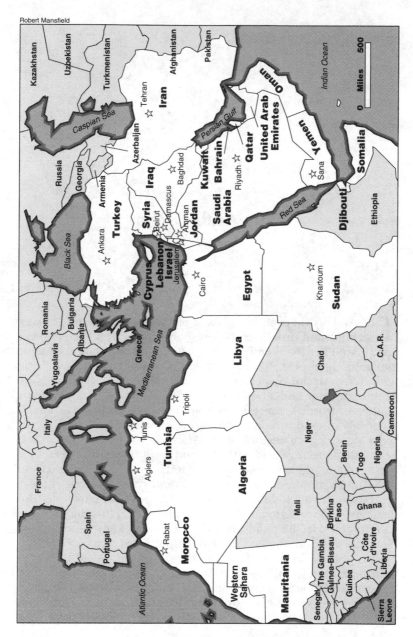

Robert Mansfield

10

intellectual discourse is, in most instances, an exercise in flattering those who matter.

This was the Arab world in which Saddam Hussein and others like him worked, conspired and bullied others on and before August 2, 1990. Brutal as Saddam Hussein's invasion of Kuwait was, it was a symptom of the chronic Arab malaise—the absence of democracy and the lopsided distribution of economic wealth.

Arab leaders, according to Nizar Qabbani, a Syrian poet, are "political dinosaurs." In some Arab countries, the leader is the state. And in large stretches of the Arab world, the ruler, whether benevolent or malevolent, acts as a shepherd, and his flocks follow him obediently. Parliaments are often rubber stamps for incumbent elites and a subtle means for co-opting the opposition. Yet there are a few promising exceptions: in Egypt, Algeria and Jordan, in particular, parliaments are developing a habit of lively debate and a degree of autonomy from the ruler.

Civil Society in the Arab World

In the Middle East unlike in the West, civil society—the clubs, organizations and groups that act as a buffer between state power and the life of the citizen—is often poorly developed. Political parties and groups, though assertive in a number of Arab countries, are vulnerable to the power of the state. In repressive Iraq, the government has gone out of its way to destroy any vestige of civil society that it cannot dominate.

Many Muslim Arabs find a voice for their demands in religious movements, which are less vulnerable to government pressures and which represent compelling indictments of the rulers' inability to meet the legitimate social and economic demands of their people. In fact, where civil society has been systematically repressed, its Islamic sector has often been uniquely successful in surviving intact. To a large degree, this explains why Islam is today the most forceful medium for the expression of political and social dissent.

The vitality of Islamic groups often stems from the simple fact that there is no competition or the political competitors have been so discredited themselves that their support is dwindling. This phenomenon is by no means limited to the Middle East. The case of the former Soviet Union is instructive. The Soviet government emasculated and tamed civil society, bringing virtually all signifi-

11

cant political and social activity under the watchful eyes of the Communist party. Only institutions with deep cultural roots, like Islam, Judaism and Russian Orthodoxy, were able to survive. Thus, as the party deteriorated and crumbled, the only opposition institutions left standing were often religious ones. What happened in the former Soviet Union was, in part, a reaffirmation of faith, but for many citizens, the driving force was not piety but the opportunity to participate in collective bodies not associated with the dead hand of communism. By the same token, the Islamic groups in the Middle East often stand for a culturally authentic and therefore congenial alternative to ineffective and heavy-handed rule.

Faced with restive and increasingly assertive populations, some governments will continue to try to rule by repression rather than concession, but others have decided to experiment with democratization. The most advanced fledgling democracy in the Arab world is Egypt, but Jordan, Algeria, Tunisia and Yemen are also moving, in fits and starts to be sure, down the same path, and the badly battered Lebanese democracy seems to be regaining its vitality. Saudi Arabia has renewed its long-standing promise to establish a *majlis al-shura* (consultative council), which would signify a modest opening in the kingdom's political system. Incipient political liberalization has been noted even in Libya. In the non-Arab states of the region—Israel, Iran and Turkey—political life is vibrant, though in each case within important limits.

There are practical reasons for the West to encourage these experiments, even though the process of achieving political pluralism will not be smooth. In fact, an opening of the political system may produce populist governments or demagogues who exacerbate tensions rather than moderate them. But, whatever their transitional excesses, governments that are more responsive to their citizens' needs must eventually balance arms budgets against social policies and address the demands of those to whom they are accountable. Aggressive wars are not easily launched in political systems where leaders must win support for their policies through a process of consultation and consensus-building. Dictators, by contrast, are free of such constraints.

A second characteristic of the Arab malaise is the accumulation of immense wealth in the hands of the ruler and his client group. Not only do authoritarian governments have a monopoly on economic power and initiative, but many Arab rulers use state funds as though they are personal bank accounts. Many leaders have accounts and investments worth tens, and in some instances, hundreds of millions of dollars. Corruption is rife. Some members of Syrian President Assad's Alawite community have amassed large fortunes and received noncompetitive contracts to engage in lucrative businesses. (The Alawites, found in Lebanon as well as Syria, are not accepted by all Muslims as adherents of Islam. They are, in effect, a sect within a sect, having developed out of Shiism. Like the Shiites, the Alawites have suffered discrimination, but through the Syrian army they have moved to political domination in Damascus.)

Saddam Hussein, trusted members of his family and cohorts from his village of Takrit, according to the CBS news program *60 Minutes,* have siphoned up to $11 billion from Iraq's oil revenues. Takrit has, in fact, provided the lion's share of the regime's insiders in Iraq. When the ruling al-Sabah family abandoned Kuwait to the invading Iraqis, the family members had at their disposal over $100 billion in cash and assets. King Fahd of Saudi Arabia has billions of dollars in his name. It is a well-known fact that Saudi and other Gulf princes pocket millions from the oil revenues of their countries, and princely *wasta* (influence) can be the key to winning a bid for a contract in Saudi Arabia.

Other Fortunes

Oil oligarchs and the Alawites and Takritis do not have a monopoly on riches. King Hussein of Jordan is considered one of the wealthiest men in the world, while Yasir Arafat, the chairman of the PLO, controls the financial levers of an organization whose cash and assets are estimated at anywhere from $2 billion to $14 billion (probably closer to $2 billion, according to *The Wall Street Journal).* Besides using money to gain loyalty and influence, Arafat also employs it as a weapon to punish opponents, as he did when he withdrew $700 million from the Arab Bank in Amman, Jordan's capital, following the worsening of his relations with King Hussein in 1986. Although Arafat has no penchant for luxuries, his total control of the public and hidden resources of the PLO has raised concern that in case he disappears, no one will know how much money there is or where it is located.

Arafat also administers an oversized and expensive bureaucracy. He oversees every detail of the day-to-day activities of the PLO, including the purchase of office equipment and the funding of petty projects. Corruption is massive, and reform-minded Palestinians routinely charge senior PLO officials with running *dakakin,* or "political shops," to buy favors, neutralize opponents and protect their political turf. There nevertheless exists a significant degree of pluralism in the PLO, and political bargaining takes place in the quasi-parliament, the Palestine National Council (PNC). The PLO was successful in helping rebuild the Palestinian community which had been shattered by the creation of Israel in 1948. Despite overwhelming odds, the organization became the institutional expression of Palestinian nationalism, with observer status at the UN, embassies in a large number of countries and widespread recognition as the legitimate voice of the Palestinians. To be sure, Arafat's pro-Iraq position during the Gulf crisis damaged the PLO, but the organization continues to enjoy the backing of the overwhelming majority of Palestinians.

Authoritarianism's Deep Roots

The governments of the Gulf have made significant progress in education and health care and in raising living standards. Moreover, they have been generous in offering financial contributions and political support to other Arabs, particularly the Palestinians. Syria and Iraq have also made impressive progress in numerous social and economic areas.

Despite these achievements, and the region's abundant human and natural resources, there has been little movement toward political reform. Even in those countries where political pluralism has started to emerge, authoritarianism still has a strong grip. There are four principal explanations for this phenomenon:

The Ottoman Legacy. First, there is the legacy of the Ottoman Empire, which ruled to a greater or lesser extent for four centuries until the end of World War I. The Ottoman Empire was heavily bureaucratic. The sultan, or sovereign, ruled ostensibly through the *askari* class, literally the military, but in practice through court officials and army officers, civil servants and *ulama,* or religious scholars. The rest of society, including all Muslim and non-Muslim subjects who paid taxes, constituted the *raaya,* or followers. Philosophically speaking, this order of rule was considered to be of divine origin and therefore immutable. While the sultan's duty was to maintain order with the help of the askar, that of the raaya was to obey and help sustain God's order. This accorded with the belief that the revealed principles of religion (i.e., Islam) stood above state and society.

The spirit of the Ottoman legacy remained after the demise of the empire. What survived in the Arab world was a political model wherein the ruler gathered all power in his hands with the support of a group of loyal officials and officers. He relied on the army as an instrument of political control, while paying little attention to the development of political institutions. The Ottoman model of rule reinforced the Arab tradition of patrimonialism and patriarchy. During the interlude of European domination, the colonial powers' contacts with the Arab world produced political and social changes, but they failed to create enduring political structures.

Political Identity. Second is the fact that for about 13 centuries, until the end of World War I, the Arabs thought of themselves primarily as Muslims. Their political loyalty belonged to Islam and to its protector, the Ottoman dynasty and state, which were the heirs and successors of the great Islamic empires of the past—the Umayyad, Abbasid and Seljuk.

With the expansion of Western influence in the latter part of the nineteenth century, the belief that society's interests are supreme began to spread in the Middle East. Along with Western economic and political penetration and the dissolution of the Ottoman Empire came the European concept of nationalism. It was seized upon by a small group of intellectuals, journalists and notables, disenchanted with the "Turkification" policies of the ruling elites in Istanbul, who molded it into a vaguely articulated ideology of Arab nationalism. This new ideology assumed the existence of one united and independent Arab nation, bound by language, culture and a shared history. While the Islamic foundation of Arab nationalism was strong, so was its tendency toward secularism, all the more so because Christians and modernizing Muslims had played a key role in its creation.

As a guide to social action, Arab nationalism never struck deep roots, and until the end of World War I the overwhelming majority of Arabs continued to identify themselves as Ottomans; some had no political identity at all.

With the Ottoman Empire gone after World War I, Arabs searched for a new identity. Partly as a result of the fragility of pan-Arab consciousness, and partly as a result of the dismemberment of the Arab territories by the British and the French, the most viable option was to identify culturally with *qawmiyyah* (Arab nationalism) but for political purposes with *wataniyyah* (local nationalism). How to reconcile the two remains a challenge and a source of friction in inter-Arab relations. Successive crises, including the 1961 breakup of Egyptian-Syrian unity and the 1967 Arab defeat by the Israelis, seriously weakened the pan-Arab idea. The Gulf war may have killed it. Some have even suggested that Arab nationalism was not killed; it committed suicide when Iraq invaded Kuwait and the Arab anti-Iraq coalition invited foreign troops to liberate Kuwait and destroy Iraq.

Whatever the destiny of Arab nationalism may be, the crisis of political identity will continue to loom large in the Arab world, reinforced on the one hand by the competing claims of secular nationalism and Islam, and on the other by ethnic and other primordial loyalties. To a great extent, this explains the absence of cohesive political communities in the Arab world. Until now, the Arabs seem to have failed to achieve what the scholar Ibn Khaldoun (1332–1406) called *asabiyya* (social cohesion), which to him was the foundation of stability, greatness and prosperity. This constitutes a serious obstacle to the emergence of democracy, since democracy presupposes the existence of a citizenry that subscribes to the principle that the interests of the larger political community should prevail.

Nonautonomous Institutions. A third explanation for the lack of movement toward political reform is the absence of autonomous institutions. The Ottoman legacy did not carry the seeds of representative government. Guilds, social groups and even the ulama did not have a corporate identity. Rather they were employed, promoted and paid by the state, and therefore never developed a social base of their own. True, there was always consultation, and the elective principle was introduced in the latter part of the nineteenth century, but real power was vested almost completely in the sovereign.

When England and France colonized the Arab lands after World War I, they imposed fragile institutions—parliaments, constitutions, modern armies and bureaucracies—on societies still wedded to patrimonialism, kinship and loyalty to a ruling dynasty. These alien institutions never took root: the political soil was not yet suitable.

A number of Arab countries did experiment with parliamentary democracy, but the experiments stalled primarily because there were no checks on the overwhelming power of the central authorities. No wonder therefore that an Arab society without independent institutions has emerged from the debris of the Ottoman Empire.

Government Dominance. Lastly, political reform is thwarted by the phenomenon of the pervasive and highly centralized government. Not only is government in the Arab world bureaucratized and militarized, it is the principal growth industry. In Egypt, Iraq and Syria, the number of government employees has increased at least ninefold over the last 20 years. If the members of the armed and security services are included, government employs more than one fourth of the working population. The same applies on a much larger scale to the oil-rich countries where every citizen is guaranteed a job as well as lavish government subsidies. Instead of drafting recruits or levying taxes to pay for the Gulf war, the Saudi government offered to forgive two years of home-mortgage payments, to discount domestic airfares and to increase grain subsidies. This was all designed to buy off dissent and create a docile and materially content society. This increased dependence on the government as a source of livelihood undermines the democratic impulse because employees of the state cannot afford to bargain over political and civil liberties. In addition to being a major source of jobs, government controls important sectors of the economy as well as natural resources.

Economic Inequality

The Gulf war underscored the painful fact that a tiny minority of Arabs enjoy riches and luxuries while the rest live in misery. According to Muhammad Tarbush, a Geneva-based Iraqi banker-scholar, only 5 percent of the Arab people are nationals of the oil-producing Gulf countries, whose aggregate GNP amounts to 55 percent of that generated by the rest of the Arab world.

Hisham Sharabi, another Arab intellectual who teaches Arab culture and history at Georgetown University, described this lop-sided situation: "Of the region's...[total population]," he wrote, "perhaps 2 percent live in luxury and splendor; some 10 percent, the small middle class, enjoy relative ease and comfort; and the majority, close to 90 percent, struggle for mere survival."

Much of this state of affairs is attributable to the mediocrity, greed and corruption of certain Arab leaders and individuals. In a recent essay, Walid Khalidi, a Palestinian research fellow at Harvard University, stated the problem in these words:

> If the congruence between the geographic distribution of wealth and demography could be said to be God-made and hence immune to critical assault, no such reprieve could be won for the man-made Western orientation of investment strategies of the oil-rich countries. And even if it is conceded that the insecurity of investment conditions in the Arab countries, no less than rational investment calculus, dictate an investment strategy oriented toward the highly industrialized Western countries, the counterargument points to the lack of proportionality between the investments <u>inside</u> and those <u>outside</u> the Arab world and to the perpetuation, at least partly by this lack, of the continued underdevelopment of the non-oil-rich Arab countries. [Emphasis original.]

At the height of the Gulf war, for example, when citizens of needy Arab states were defending Saudi Arabia, a Saudi prince invested $590 million in preferred stock of Citicorp, owner of the largest commercial bank in the United States. Many Arabs found both the deed and the timing distasteful and distressing.

After the Iraqi invasion, there was widespread sentiment among many Arabs and non-Arab sympathizers that fighting a war in order to restore an oppressive regime was wrong and that the economic situation would have to change. Some called for a new order anchored in an equitable distribution of surplus wealth among Arab economies. One ambitious proposal called for pooling Gulf riches in an irrevocable trust that would benefit all Muslims and thus help win back the alienated who had rallied behind Saddam Hussein.

So far, these calls have fallen on deaf ears. The Gulf countries rewarded those who took their side, and punished those who opposed them or sat on the fence by cutting off financial aid. Among the victims have been the Palestinians, the Jordanians, the Yemenis and the North Africans. Saddam Hussein claimed he was the Robin Hood of the wretched. Although he was defeated, to the millions who are still suffering, Saddam Hussein's populist critique of the Arab establishment still rings true.

Iraq's Invasion of Kuwait

Why did Saddam Hussein invade Kuwait? Many interpretations of his motives have been advanced. The theories tend to fall into two categories: one stresses his brutality and greed for money; the other attributes the invasion to a conspiracy. Some of his Arab supporters claim he was the victim of a plan orchestrated by the United States and Israel after the August 1988 cease-fire between Iran and Iraq. According to this view, the purpose of the conspiracy was to disarm Iraq, leaving Israel the dominant military power in the region. In furtherance of the plan, the United States allegedly led Saddam Hussein to believe, less than two weeks before Iraq's seizure of Kuwait, that Washington would not respond with force if Saddam Hussein invaded that country.

A number of elements undoubtedly entered into President Hussein's calculations in the few months before his invasion of Kuwait. As to the conspiracy theories, only history can provide the answers. There is little question, however, that his personality and outlook directly affected his decisions.

Saddam Hussein, along with some members of his inner circle, views with deep suspicion everything around him. Because of his underground and conspiratorial activities ever since the beginning

19

of his political career, secretiveness and distrust of outsiders pervade his thinking and behavior. This frame of mind was probably one of the chief factors that influenced his decision to invade. Wittingly or unwittingly, the Kuwaiti government reinforced his suspicions. Besides exceeding the oil-production quota set up by the cartel of oil producers, the Organization of Petroleum Exporting Countries (OPEC), Kuwait was "stealing" oil from the Rumaila field, a 50-mile-long banana-shaped oil reservoir, the bulk of which lies under Iraq. From Iraq's perspective, Kuwait's overproduction and pumping of oil from Rumaila was tantamount to an act of economic war, orchestrated with foreign powers in order to weaken Iraq. President Hussein's statement at the Baghdad Arab summit on May 30, 1990, and the memorandum of his foreign minister, Tariq Aziz, to the secretary-general of the Arab League on July 15, 1990, made it clear how seriously he viewed these matters. (The league was founded in 1945 to promote the unity of Arab states.)

The Iraqi debt crisis may also have played a role in Saddam Hussein's decision to invade. Iraq emerged from its eight-year war with Iran with a staggering debt of $80 billion, according to Phebe Marr, the National Defense University expert on Iraq. Nearly half of the debt was owed to the Gulf Cooperation Council (GCC) countries (Bahrain, Kuwait, Oman, Qatar, Saudi Arabia and the United Arab Emirates), including $4 billion to Kuwait. Kuwait kept reminding the Iraqi president of his debt which infuriated him, since he felt that Iraq had sacrificed not only money but the lives of its sons to defend the Gulf countries against "Khomeiniism." On an earlier occasion, in 1985, when Iranian operatives had tried to assassinate the emir of Kuwait, the Iraqis had retaliated against Iran and suffered 1,500 casualties. Iraq's sacrifices led Saddam Hussein to believe that his country was entitled to forgiveness of the entire debt owed to the GCC, as well as the additional $30 billion in credits the Gulf states had provided during the war with Iran. At an Arab summit in Jidda, Saudi Arabia, on July 31, 1990, Kuwait and Iraq failed to bridge their differences. There are contending versions of how forthcoming Kuwait was willing to be in meeting Iraq's demands. According to one account, by the journalist Pierre Salinger, Kuwait offered Iraq a loan of $9 billion, while other sources claim Kuwait was willing to offer Iraq no more than a $500,000 gift.

Iraqi President Saddam Hussein shaking hands with soldiers somewhere in Kuwait on January 15, 1991, hours before the UN deadline for Iraq's withdrawal.

Reuters/Bettmann

Other factors, both ideological and tactical, may have contributed to Saddam Hussein's decision to seize Kuwait. His claim that Kuwait was an integral part of Iraq mirrored the position of his predecessors, most notably King Ghazi, who advocated the absorption of Kuwait by Iraq in 1937, and Abdel-Karim Qasim, who laid the same claim to Kuwait in July 1961. The claim was based on the argument that Kuwait had once been a district of the Basra *wilayah* (province) in Ottoman times, a status which was terminated by the 1899 Kuwaiti-British agreement which made Kuwait a virtual British protectorate. On the tactical level, Iraq's seizure of Kuwait promised to expand the Iraqi coastline on the Gulf from a 36-mile strip to more than 300 miles.

In brief, these were the factors that motivated Saddam Hussein to act on August 2, 1990. How Saddam Hussein appraised the risks of his invasion, one can only speculate. Given his poor understanding of the outside world, especially the United States, he may well have felt that the Americans would march to the abyss of war and lack the will to go forward, although Saddam Hussein and his confidants concluded early on that President George Bush was intent on pursuing the crisis to war. (Authoritative interviews with leading Iraqi players, like former Foreign Minister Tariq Aziz, indicate that

21

Iraq anticipated an American response but thought it could out-maneuver the Americans.) He had an exaggerated view of the persistence of the Vietnam syndrome, American disillusionment with foreign involvement. He apparently assumed that any warlike moves by the United States would send shudders through the American public and tie the President's hands. He may also have calculated that since the Soviets were not implicated in the invasion, the U.S. government would condemn it loudly but not act. The Iraqi leader may have believed further that if the United States did attack Iraq, the Arab masses would overthrow their leaders and rally behind Iraq. Whatever his calculations, his decisions from the onset of the crisis showed not only that he misunderstood the consequences of his acts but that he is a poor strategist. His advisers and colleagues did not take issue with him: the evidence shows that they told him exactly what he wanted to hear, perhaps because they shared their leader's misconceptions or simply because it was safer to agree than to dissent.

The UN and the Gulf Crisis

One of Saddam Hussein's most egregious miscalculations was in failing to understand the dramatic shift that had occurred at the UN.

On August 2, 1990, when Iraq's army crashed into Kuwait, it was not possible to foresee the many twists and turns that the crisis would take, but it was clear from the very onset of the crisis that a successful counter to Iraqi aggression would involve the UN. Even for the United States, the political and economic costs of going it alone were too high and the benefits of working through the UN were too obvious for the crisis to have played out differently. This is not to say that the Bush Administration was of one mind regarding the UN's role. There were moments when the go-it-alone advocates might have carried the day had it not been for the pressures of outside powers, particularly the Soviet Union. Thus in August, when the United States was moving unilaterally toward the creation of a naval blockade, it was a Soviet demurral that helped convince the U.S. Administration to secure the blessings of the UN. The result was the Security Council's adoption of Resolution 665, which authorized the use of maritime forces to implement the embargo of Iraq.

Since mid-1987 the Security Council has been functioning as

Egypt's President Hosni Mubarak, at a news conference in Alexandria on August 28, 1990, urged Saddam Hussein to accept a peaceful solution to the Gulf crisis.

Reuters/Bettmann

the collegial body anticipated in the UN Charter rather than as a rhetorical battleground for great and not-so-great powers. The five permanent members—Britain, China, France, the U.S.S.R. and the United States—had begun coordinating their policies during the Iran-Iraq War. That war ended in a cease-fire within the framework of Security Council Resolution 598.

The former Soviet Union deserves significant credit for fostering the new mood of cooperation and activism at the UN. In 1987 Soviet President Mikhail S. Gorbachev began emphasizing the UN's potential role in conflict resolution. Moscow embraced the UN across-the-board as the most effective actor to stem and solve Third World conflicts. The Soviet policy shifts were followed by changes in U.S. policy toward the UN that have brought the world body back to center stage. The earlier U.S. mistrust and distaste for the UN, which was so evident from 1981 to 1987, has been replaced by a pragmatic U.S. willingness to exploit UN mechanisms for mitigating regional conflicts. After prolonged episodes of ideological axe-grinding by U.S. ambassadors at the UN, the United States returned to the motif of quiet diplomacy with an emphasis on the UN's positive peacekeeping and peacemaking roles. Early in his presidency, Bush took steps to demonstrate his commitment to the institution that he had served as U.S. ambassador in the early 1970s.

Throughout the Gulf crisis, the Soviet representative voted

against his country's erstwhile ally, Iraq, overruling some of the military and area specialists in the foreign ministry who were intent on preserving the relationship with Iraq.

No event more dramatically symbolized the changed international climate and the end of the cold war than the November 29, 1990, meeting of the UN Security Council. The Soviet Union joined the United States, Britain, France and eight other Security Council members in approving Resolution 678, which authorized the use of "all necessary means" to bring an end to the Iraqi seizure of Kuwait. (Yemen and Cuba voted against the resolution, and China, consistently the most reticent permanent member, abstained.) Of the 12 resolutions passed between August 2, 1990, when the Security Council condemned the Iraqi invasion, and the approval of Resolution 678, there were 5 unanimous ballots, 2 with 14 positive votes and 4 with 13 positive votes, and Resolution 678 passed with 12 yes votes, 2 noes and 1 abstention. The unprecedented coupling, in a Security Council resolution, of the three words "all necessary means" marked a turning point in the history of the UN. Despite the elliptical diplomatic vocabulary, the resolution put the stamp of international legality on a sweeping use of military power to reverse a transparent act of aggression. Thus, when the United States and its allies launched their offensive against Iraqi forces in and around Kuwait, the international community's imprimatur was figuratively emblazoned on every bomb.

The passage of the historic resolution would not have been possible had there not been undisguised aggression, the absence of a unified Arab response to the crisis, and the resolve, indeed obduracy, of the United States as well as Britain in denying Iraq any gain from its aggression. An unanswered question is whether there could have been an "Arab solution" and, if so, whether the United States intentionally sabotaged it. According to some journalists, the United States applied pressure, particularly on Egyptian President Hosni Mubarak, to condemn the Iraqi invasion. (Mubarak privately cited "tremendous pressure.") Having denounced the invasion, Egypt could not gracefully withdraw its troops from the coalition. In journalist Milton Viorst's account in *The New Yorker*, Saddam Hussein had reached an early agreement with Saudi King Fahd that Iraq would withdraw its troops from Kuwait but would retain the Rumaila oil field and the islands of Bubiyan and Warba.

Arab Systems of Government

Before examining the various Arab reactions to the Gulf crisis and its effect on inter-Arab politics, it is helpful to take a look at the political systems of the leading players.

In terms of political organization, Arab states share a number of similarities, but their political systems are not identical. The level of political participation and the methods of political control and legitimation vary from state to state. Generally speaking, Arab governments fall into one of three groups: (1) single-party authoritarian systems, (2) oil oligarchies, and (3) semicompetitive multiparty systems.

This chapter deals with the basic characteristics of each group and the prospects for political reform. We will look at seven countries—Iraq, Syria, Saudi Arabia, Egypt, Jordan, Algeria and Tunisia.

Single-Party Authoritarian Systems

The outstanding examples of single-party authoritarian governments are **Iraq** and **Syria**. In many respects, the two governments approximate the Soviet model before Gorbachev's reforms. One major difference is the absence of the Marxist philosophy of class warfare.

The Iraqi and Syrian regimes are highly institutionalized. The Baath (Renaissance) party is the dominant party in Baghdad, the Iraqi capital, and Damascus, Syria's capital. Each of the regimes claims to be the authentic custodian of Baathism, an ideology that advocates the creation of a single Arab nation as the ultimate expression of freedom, progress and glory. It also stresses egalitarianism and the redistribution of wealth.

Iraq

In the case of Iraq, power is concentrated in the Regional Command of the Baath party, the Revolutionary Command Council (RCC), and high-level state bureaucracies. There is considerable overlap of personnel among the three.

The party organization is structured in the form of a pyramid. At the top is the Regional Command, chaired by Saddam Hussein, which exercises control at the national level. Next are the area commands, each headed by a senior party loyalist. Below them are the branches, divisions, sections and cells. The sections encompass small urban quarters or villages, and recruit new members and execute party policy. The cells have a small number of active members and operate at the neighborhood level.

In practice, the most important function of the party is to discipline its members and mold them into an effective and loyal political force. As an institution, the Baath party in Iraq is deeply intrusive. Since it took power in 1968, it has succeeded in welding into an effective unit not only its supporters among the professionals, the military, the middle class and the intellectuals of Iraq, but it has also tried to recruit followers in other Arab countries, most notably Lebanon, Mauritania and the Arab states of the Gulf. In Iraq proper, the Baath party created a formidable social base of some 1.5 million supporters and sympathizers (nearly 11 percent of the population), a figure which only partially overlaps with the nearly 1 million state workers. Despite this achievement, the party has neither attracted nor mobilized the urban lower class or the rural population. This may partially explain why the marginally modernized people of northern and southern Iraq joined the insurrection against Saddam Hussein after the cessation of hostilities at the end of February 1991.

Functioning parallel to and overlapping with the Baath party organization is the RCC. Originally set up in 1968, the RCC usually consists of more than a dozen members. Continuity of membership is not a main feature of the council, partly as a result of power struggles, but also because Saddam Hussein has been hesitant to keep the same people in top positions lest they develop their own power base. The sectarian composition of the RCC leadership has also changed. In June 1982, for example, the balance shifted in favor of the Shiites; earlier it had overwhelmingly favored the Sunnis, members of the other major branch of the Islamic religion who predominate in the Arab world but are outnumbered by Shiites in Iraq and Iran. The reason for the broadening of Shiite representation was Saddam Hussein's desire to integrate the Shiite majority into the Iraqi body politic, thus preempting Khomeini's plan to incite the Shiites to rebel against Iraq's Sunni leadership. As Phebe Marr observes, Sunni dominance in Iraq "has not been based on a sectarian policy but is related to the fact that the core of the original leadership elite originated in the central area of the country where Arab Sunnis predominate."

The 1970 provisional constitution of Iraq and its 1973 amendments refer to the RCC as the highest legislative body, entrusted with the supreme authority to oversee all foreign and domestic policies. In actuality, the RCC is a pliable state organ with little independent power. The same is true of the party and its regional command. Almost absolute power is vested in a hierarchical structure headed by the Iraqi president himself.

Early in 1991 authoritative sources reported that Saddam Hussein's closest associate was Lt. Gen. Hussein Kamil Hassan, a cousin and son-in-law who hails from the president's native Takrit region. In the tumultuous period following the Iraqi defeat and expulsion from Kuwait, the general was appointed minister of defense. But, by November 1991, Saddam Hussein had dismissed him and replaced him with another cousin amidst rumors of dissension and even gunfights within the inner circle.

The concentration of so much power in such a small group, with a narrow geographic base and the balance of power overwhelmingly in favor of the Takritis, has created resentment among many Iraqis, especially the educated middle class.

Although Saddam Hussein decisively dominates the power structure, he has had to cope with other groups and forces. Working parallel with, but subservient to, the RCC and the Baath party hierarchy are the unions, the military, the Popular Army and the security apparatus. The top echelons of the unions are staffed by Baath party loyalists who were elected to their positions through party support. This has enabled the party to exercise strong control over the unions. The same cannot be said about the army. Saddam Hussein has been able to some extent to subordinate the military to civilian control, but the periodic purges and personnel shuffles at the highest levels within the military indicate that the regime's control of the military is far from complete. The Republican Guard has been the mainstay of Saddam Hussein's influence over the officer corps, and the intelligence service, the *mukhabarat,* is the eyes and ears of the regime. To ensure maximum control and loyalty, the regime has created a multilayered secret service apparatus staffed with people blindly loyal to the president. According to most observers, the mukhabarat played a critical role in helping Saddam Hussein amass power.

Like all politicians, Saddam Hussein had to inculcate a sense of legitimacy, or legal status, in order to secure obedience and conformity. Whereas in democratic systems the right to rule is acquired through periodic competitive elections, in Iraq it is based on political institutions and ideology. The Iraqi regime's ideological legitimacy rests on its declared fidelity to pan-Arab concerns, with Arabism and the Palestine question heading the list. In an attempt to outmaneuver the Arab governments aligned against him during the Gulf crisis, Saddam Hussein linked the withdrawal of Iraqi forces from Kuwait to Israel's withdrawal from occupied Palestinian and Arab land. This endeared the Iraqi leader to many, though not all, Palestinians, especially those living in Jordan and under Israeli occupation. Besides causing immense difficulties for the Palestinians in a number of Arab countries, their support of Saddam Hussein may also lead to a backlash against them in Iraq: Iraqis who oppose Saddam Hussein may seek revenge against those who sympathized with him.

As far as institutional legitimacy is concerned, Saddam Hussein tried to achieve this by his very limited opening up of the political process. This took the form of an elected National Assembly dominated by the RCC, and the manipulated election of representatives serving in professional unions and in party branches.

After the Gulf war, Saddam Hussein promised to introduce political reforms in an attempt to win over the Iraqi people and deflect external pressure. But his sacking on September 13, 1991,

Syrian President Hafez al-Assad, influenced both by personal animosity toward Saddam Hussein and power politics, placed his government in the anti-Iraq camp during the Gulf crisis.

Reuters/Bettmann

of Prime Minister Sa'doun Hammadi, who was widely viewed as relatively moderate and was appointed while the regime was still reeling from its defeat, indicates that President Hussein was insincere about relaxing his political grip on Iraq.

Syria

Syria shares with Iraq a number of key characteristics. At the apex of the power structure is President Assad, a man of humble origin, who methodically made his way to the top through the military. He was defense minister until he launched the coup that made him prime minister in 1970 and then president in 1971. Assad may rival Saddam Hussein in ruthlessness, but his style of politics is totally different. Whereas President Hussein is the rash brawler, Assad is the cautious, wily fox. Syria has been enmeshed in the Lebanese civil war since 1976. But Assad's move-and-pause strategy and his awareness of the delicate calculus of costs and benefits enabled him to keep Syria away from any fatal ventures or entrapments.

Assad's institutional base is the Baath party. The party's highest organs are the Regional Command and a looser structure called the Central Committee. Assad is the secretary-general of the party. He heads the Regional Command, which consists of 21 senior cadres who supervise the various divisions of the party as well as the Syrian government itself. While the Regional Command makes the ultimate decisions on domestic and foreign matters, the Central Committee provides a forum for consultation between the Regional Command and the local party bodies. Although it is in Assad's nature to consult, he usually has the final say.

Around the party Assad has gathered a hard core of five institutions, all subservient to him and all designed to block the emergence of a viable opposition. These are the People's Council, whose 173 members were elected by universal suffrage in 1972; the National Progressive Front, a party-dominated body whose membership consists of the Baath party, the Communist party, the Arab Socialist Movement and other small political groupings; local councils representing Syria's 14 governorates, each having a governor who acts as an instrument of the central government; a pervasive security apparatus consisting of numerous agencies, each one spying on the others; and the heavily armed defense brigades, who not only guard key government buildings and provide security for the regime but are an offensive arm which the Syrian government can use against its enemies.

These political bodies were intended to provide the Assad regime with legitimacy—that is, to create a semblance of public accountability, political pluralism and citizen participation in state institutions. The Baath party has been called a "clan masquerading as a political party," and the other institutions are no different. They all ensure that Syrians obey their rulers or at least refrain from revolt.

✳ ✳ ✳

The Iraqi and Syrian governments could take one of three approaches to political reform. They could abdicate power, resist any change or make some limited cosmetic reforms. The first is the least likely: in most parts of the Arab world, the leader who surrenders the reins of power does not retire to a think tank, a major corporation or a university. Either he is killed or forced into exile. Little wonder therefore that the undeclared slogan of Arab leaders is "rule or die." Unlike in pre-1989 Eastern Europe, there is no distant master to push the reform button. Moreover, all significant internal opponents have been suppressed, co-opted or forced to flee. The secret police is omnipresent. As Saddam Hussein observed to a British journalist in 1971, "With our party methods, there is no chance for anyone who disagrees with us to jump on a couple of tanks and overthrow the government. These methods have gone." Thus pressure from within the regime to force change at the top is unlikely. This is especially true in the case of Syria, where there is no insurgency and no massive destruction resulting from a suicidal foreign policy. Even if the military were to mount a successful coup, it is by no means clear that a new government would look very different from the one it replaced.

The second option is to perpetuate the present state of affairs, and this is the most likely path that the incumbents in Baghdad and Damascus will follow. But if the wind of change blows, as it did in Eastern Europe, then the Iraqi and Syrian governments may be forced to choose the third path. In the short run, the most that could be expected from the Baath political regimes would be some form of elections and the emergence of a fragile multiparty system controlled by a troika consisting of the army, the party and the secret police.

In Iraq, the destruction wrought by the U.S.-led coalition and the insurrections that followed the war may open up possibilities for change. There is a chance—but a remote one—that a junta of senior Baathist generals or officers or even a government of national reconciliation might emerge, but either course presumes that Saddam Hussein is removed from power. Should Saddam Hussein stay in power, then the likelihood of change or even national reconciliation will be small at best.

Irrespective of how great the need for reform, it is important not to underestimate the tasks facing a political leader in either country. The ethnic and religious diversity of Iraqis, together with the conflict between city and tribe, has created an Iraqi identity that is part supranational, part subnational. This applies to Syria as well, though not to the same degree. As a consequence, the weakening of central authority may loose an array of divisive forces. The recent experiences of the Soviet Union and Yugoslavia are instructive of the fragility of states held together with generous rations of coercion.

Oil Oligarchies

The oil oligarchies—Saudi Arabia and the other Gulf sheikhdoms of Bahrain, Kuwait, Oman, Qatar and the United Arab Emirates—are still dynastic structures based on birth and lineage. In all of these governments the head of the dynasty, the most senior member of the ruling family, stands at the center of the political process. His entourage consists of the more prominent members of his family or household, who occupy the other key positions of power. Members of the leading commoner families may hold important administrative positions, but they rarely reach the pinnacle of power; if they do, it is either because they are closely allied with the head of the dynasty or he has chosen to adopt them politically.

In general, these dynastic governments seek to achieve legitimacy and control in two ways: (1) through Arab tribal customs, Islamic institutions and law, and through the distribution of economic benefits to their subjects and granting them direct access to the ruler; or (2) by the establishment of statelike institutions, including a cabinet, a national assembly, a defense force, public security and a patronage network anchored upon tribalism.

Saudi Arabia

In many ways Saudi Arabia provides a representative example of this system of rule. Although it is a very closed system compared to the rest—and can be as puzzling to outsiders as the plot of a complex detective novel—it is similar in many ways to the other oligarchies.

The power structure in Saudi Arabia is three-tiered. The core group is the king and his entourage of princes who articulate national policy and who are, for all practical purposes, the actual power elite. A second layer consists of court staff who advise the rulers, and a third, state ministries and departments that carry out bureaucratic duties and implement decisions. It is difficult to determine whether the structure of authority is cohesive or fragmented. While consensus-building seems to be central to the Saudi policy process, many observers have indicated that key decisions in Saudi Arabia result from a process of consultation among the king and the most powerful princes, with the king having the final say in high policy matters. And either the king or the crown prince meets with religious leaders on a regular basis in order to gauge their opinion or win their support. Understanding Saudi Arabia's position on strategic issues, therefore, is largely a matter of identifying and understanding the perceptions and preferences of King Fahd.

Fahd's legitimacy, like his predecessors', is grounded in his descent from the Saud family, his selection by consensus, his claim that he is the protector and propagator of Islam, and his concern for the welfare of the nation. In the wider Arab arena, the Saudi monarch has embraced the Palestinian cause and the Arab quest for an end to Israel's occupation of Arab land. He has done so both out of principle and because these values touch a responsive chord across the Arab world.

By supplying almost unconditional foreign aid to Arab governments and movements, the Saudi royal family secured for itself an insurance policy against opposition from Arab elites across its borders. At the same time the royal family has consciously avoided taking the lead in foreign policy (at least it did until the onset of the Gulf crisis), preferring instead to build consensus among the key Arab players. It is motivated by an awareness of the country's limitations and vulnerabilities, and by a desire to protect the family's legitimacy.

To further consolidate its power, the Saudi royal family created a number of institutions, among them the General Intelligence Directorate, which is responsible for intelligence gathering, the Committee for the Propagation of Virtue and the Prevention of Vice, which is intended to project an image of moral rectitude, and the National Guard, which is designed to counterbalance the regular army and ensure the safety of the regime. The National Guard, which is manned by tribal levies and whose members receive cash and land in return for their loyalty, is routinely involved in tribal, political and internal security functions.

In the absence of political parties and organized opposition, public opinion in Saudi Arabia is expressed through traditional interest groups such as tribes, families and professional organizations, including the semiofficial Saudi Chamber of Commerce and Industry. An open-door forum, the majlis, provides Saudi citizens with the opportunity to express their opinions or grievances to senior Saudi officials. This forum of tribal "democracy" used to be attended fairly regularly by Saudi monarchs until King Faysal was assassinated at a majlis session by one of his nephews in March 1975. This institution, which exists in all the Arab countries of the Gulf and is unique to them, gives citizens direct access to their rulers.

✳ ✳ ✳

In estimating the prospects for democratic change in the oil oligarchies, much depends on how one defines democracy. If democracy entails a high level of political participation in the selection of leaders and a meaningful level of civil and political liberties, then the chances for democracy in the short run are poor. This is due to the traditional nature of the regimes and the absence of real participation. But if by democracy is meant a more open political system, one which allows for greater political liberty and especially the phased introduction to the royal majlis of elected members alongside royally appointed ones, then the prospects are better, especially in the small states of the Gulf.

In Saudi Arabia, certainly the most socially conservative Arab state, there have long been pressures from middle-class professionals for the regime to provide an outlet for popular participation in decisionmaking. Since 1962 there have been periodic promises to establish a consultative council, but the promises have never been fulfilled. Typically, the proposal is dusted off during a moment of popular discontent and then promptly shelved for a few more years. In November 1990, in the midst of the Gulf crisis and on the heels of a pledge by the Kuwaiti royal family to restore parliamentary life in the emirate, the promise was revived. Just as the Kuwaiti emir's commitment remains unfulfilled, so does King Fahd's, although in November 1991 he told reporters he was putting the finishing touches on the council. Thus, nearly 30 years after it was first announced, the council may come into existence. But rather than being a precursor to parliamentary representation, as some Saudi liberals hope, the council will probably be a conservative body more likely to stifle than to instill change.

As the protector of the two holiest cities of Islam, King Fahd is especially sensitive to any charge that he is placing the sanctity or purity of Mecca and Medina in jeopardy. Although the ulama of the puritanical Wahhabi sect do not rule in Saudi Arabia, they are keenly concerned with the state of public morals, and they are a conservative bulwark for the monarch and the regime. In effect, a challenge to the regime's Islamic probity is a challenge to its very legitimacy. Hence, King Fahd had to be sensitive to conservative grumbling over his agreement to permit the predominantly non-Muslim and U.S.-led anti-Iraq alliance to deploy in the kingdom.

Given an opportunity to demonstrate his credentials as the upholder of the faith, King Fahd grabbed it. This opportunity came on November 6, 1990, when some four dozen Saudi women audaciously dismissed their drivers in Riyadh, the nation's capital, and drove their own cars, thus violating the informal but well-known ban on women driving cars. The regime reacted harshly, ostracizing the participants and suspending several from teaching positions. The Supreme Council of Islamic Research lent support to the king with a *fatwa*, or authoritative religious opinion, which found that "women should not be allowed to drive motor vehicles as the *Sharia* [religious law] instructs that things that degrade or harm the dignity of women must be prevented."

Later, in May 1991, the ulama, in a move that was widely interpreted as an attempt to collect for their wartime sufferance of the regime's admitting Western troops to the kingdom as well as to counter the entreaties of liberal Saudis, presented a memorandum to King Fahd urging him to make a series of conservative reforms. These included the creation of an ulama-dominated parliament, application of consistent punishments for corruption, and the stricter application of Islamic law. The conservative reforms have not been applied, and there is little doubt that political life in Saudi Arabia will continue to be the exclusive preserve of the regime, not its citizens.

In Kuwait it is likely that the emir will decide to preserve the old system. However, the emir and his retinue will have to adjust to the emergence of a newly assertive and militant Kuwaiti opposition, which resisted the Iraqi occupiers. Kuwait will be a closely watched bellwether in the Gulf, and not all of the spectators will be cheering for political liberalization. The test will come in October 1992, when parliamentary elections are scheduled.

So far, judging by the composition of the Kuwaiti cabinet and the flouting of the demands of the opposition, the emir is determined to keep all political power in his family's hands. Moreover, judging by human-rights violations and the torture and killing of non-Kuwaitis, one can anticipate a continuation of acts of vengeance against foreigners on the pretext that some of them collaborated with the Iraqis. This should come as no surprise: only five years ago, the elites debated the wisdom of having granted citizenship to indigenous Kuwaiti Shiites and even considered removing them from sensitive positions in the army, the police and the oil industry.

It is not inconceivable that the Gulf governments in general, and Saudi Arabia in particular, may resort to violence to quell any real or potential dissent and opposition from within or from the outside. In the aftermath of the war, these governments may feel embarrassingly weak and compromised by having relied on foreign powers.

Semicompetitive Multiparty Systems

Egypt in Africa, **Jordan** in the Arab East, and **Algeria** and **Tunisia** in North Africa all have semicompetitive, multiparty systems. Unlike the single-party authoritarian regimes and the oil oligarchies, they allow a fair level of political pluralism. Egypt is ahead of the rest, and the January 1992 coup d'état in Algeria poses a significant question about the fate of liberalization in that country.

Egypt

Much has been written about the political system of Egypt. With the possible exception of Israel, no Middle Eastern country has received as much attention. Some writers have compared Egypt's leaders, since the overthrow of the monarchy in July 1952, to the ancient pharaohs, whose vision determined the country's political and economic course. (See Muhammad Hasanayn Haykal, *Autumn of Fury.*) Others have characterized the leaders according to social class. Thus Nasser (1952–70), Sadat (1970–81) and Mubarak (1981–), who came from the middle class, are said to have advanced middle-class interests. (See John Waterbury, *The Egypt of Nasser and Sadat: The Political Economy of Two Regimes.*) Other specialists have portrayed Egypt as a pluralist society that is a mirror both of Egypt and of the Arab world, a society that openly debates issues of individual and national concern. (See Fouad Ajami, *The Arab Predicament: Arab Political Thought and Practice Since 1967.*) Still others see the military elite, the "men on horseback," dominating the Egyptian political system. (See Amos Perlmutter, *Egypt: The Praetorian State.*)

Egypt's political system is probably a blend of all four characteristics, with the possible exception of the last. The Egyptian military's influence in politics remains significant but is no longer pervasive. Since the 1952 revolution, the government has been progressively demilitarized. Senior officers no longer move effortlessly into secure positions in the senior bureaucracy, and there is little question about the military's subordination to political authority. The loyalty of the army remains critical to the stability of the regime, however.

Egypt has a republican form of government headed by the president and his party, the National Democratic party (NDP). Other political parties, such as the Wafd, the Socialist Labor party, the Socialist Liberal party, the National Progressive Unionist party, and the Muslim Brotherhood, exist but they are routinely muzzled in the name of national security. A 458-seat parliament called the People's Assembly nominates the president. He is then confirmed by a popular referendum conducted by the ministry of the interior. In addition to appointing all 31 cabinet members, the president has the constitutional authority to appoint the 26 provincial governors, the 12 university chancellors, and a third of the consultative council, which is equivalent to an upper house of parliament. He also has the authority to issue presidential decrees that acquire the force of law once approved by the People's Assembly.

The current president, Mubarak, hails from an obscure rural background. He rose to power through the military and became commander of the air force. His predecessor, President Sadat, appointed him vice-president after the 1973 October war. Sadat's assassination on October 6, 1981, thrust Mubarak into the presidency. In 1987, a popular referendum renewed his term of office for another six years.

Mubarak has used a variety of techniques to legitimize his rule. On the foreign policy front, he enhanced Egypt's stature by returning it to the Arab fold while maintaining a separate peace treaty with Israel. He also positioned himself as an advocate of moderation by rejecting radical pan-Arabism and encouraging Washington to take account of Arab and Palestinian interests. More recently, Mubarak's support for the U.S.-led campaign to liberate Kuwait brought Egypt closer to the United States and the oil-rich Arab countries, thus securing much needed financial aid.

Egypt's peace with Israel and its alliance with the United States and its conservative Arab allies did not go unchallenged. Opposition parties, including the Islamic fundamentalists and the secular leftists, were highly critical of Mubarak. On balance, however, he has managed to pursue his foreign policy with the support of his party, which controls parliament, and with large infusions of foreign aid.

On the domestic front, Mubarak discarded the flamboyant and dictatorial style of his predecessor and adopted a low-key and cautious style tailored to neutralize potentially hostile groups, including the pro-Sadat elite and the Islamic fundamentalists. Moreover, in an attempt to preempt the opposition, the Egyptian president liberalized Egypt's election laws, allowing independent candidates to run for parliament. The Mubarak regime has also tolerated the existence of an opposition press and has rejected the cult of personality favored by Saddam Hussein, President Assad and, to a great degree, Mubarak's predecessor.

These liberalizing measures notwithstanding, the Egyptian president and his ruling NDP, which won 348 of the 444 seats contested in the 1990 People's Assembly elections, have a near monopoly on power over the political system. The revised election law stipulates that in order for a party to get any seats in parliament it must win at least 8 percent of the national vote—a stipulation that decisively favors the government party. More important still, the reelection of the incumbent president is guaranteed by virtue of his party's control of the People's Assembly. The interior ministry oversees the elections and the referendum that confirms a president, and the government gives financial incentives to senior military officers to assure their loyalty. It is understandable why the opposition complains about sham elections and perpetual presidential control.

Jordan

Jordan is another example of a semicompetitive multiparty system. Its government is similar to Egypt's in some respects, different in others. Unlike Egypt, which is a republic with relatively long experience with democratic experimentation and its ups and downs, Jordan is a limited constitutional monarchy that has only recently embarked on a process of democratization. The Jordanian monarch has wide powers. The country's constitution not only vests executive power in him; it also grants him considerable legislative responsibilities, including the powers to dissolve parliament and declare war. In making decisions, the king draws on a variety of

After meeting with King Hussein of Jordan, seen here in
Kennebunkport, Maine, with Secretary of State James A. Baker 3d
on August 16, 1990, President George Bush announced
that Jordan would abide by UN sanctions.

sources, notably the council of ministers and, more importantly, a
group of loyal advisers that includes his brother, Crown Prince
Hassan, and his uncle, Zayd ibn Shakir, the commander of the Jordanian
armed forces.

The bedrock of support for the monarchy is the security network.
It is an intrusive service, consisting of the army intelligence, the
police and the General Intelligence Directorate, though benign
when compared to the systems in Syria and Iraq. In addition there
are the Royal Guards, a select army unit composed of bedouin loyalists,
and the army itself, which plays the dual role of protecting the
monarchy and defending the country. Indeed the army is the backbone
of the monarchy in Jordan and has traditionally defended it
against both domestic and foreign threats. To ensure the loyalty of
the officer corps, bedouins who belong to cohesive and politically
reliable tribes are assigned key senior-level positions.

King Hussein has used a variety of techniques to legitimize his
rule. Ideologically, he has embraced the Palestine cause and subscribed
to the principles of Arab unity and Arab nationalism. Of all
the monarchs in the Arab world, King Hussein has been the stron-

gest advocate of Arab nationalism, at least verbally. His family claims descent from the Prophet Muhammad, and his great grandfather, Sharif Hussein ibn Ali, was widely regarded as having led the Arab nationalist revolt against the Ottoman Empire during World War I. (He was in fact a staunch supporter of the Ottomans and reluctantly embraced Arab nationalism for political reasons.) In a similar sense, King Hussein's adoption of the Palestine cause was as much a function of realpolitik as it was of ideological conviction. For the sake of both the nation and the Hashemite dynasty, King Hussein covets the return of the West Bank, with its precious prize, East Jerusalem.

The Jordanian king created or has tolerated a variety of institutions for the purpose of legitimizing his rule. There is a quasi-democratic parliament, with an upper House of Notables appointed by the king, and a lower House of Deputies whose members are elected. Women, who obtained the franchise in 1973, were allowed to vote for the first time in March 1984. Through cash handouts and other incentives, the Jordanian government has co-opted not only a number of politicians and intellectuals but also the army. In April 1978, the king appointed 60 prominent citizens to the National Consultative Council (NCC), an advisory body. His purpose was to accommodate reform-minded groups and individuals who were calling for greater democratic freedom. Even before the Jordanian government lifted the ban on political parties in 1989, it allowed interest groups such as trade unions, charitable societies and religious organizations, most notably the Muslim Brotherhood, some latitude in expressing their views and lobbying for reform. In April 1990, the king established a 60-member royal committee representing various shades of political opinion. Its principal function was to draw up a national reconciliation charter that would set political guidelines and restructure the relationship between the king, the cabinet and the parliament.

According to most observers, King Hussein is an astute, intelligent and flexible politician who does not burn his bridges, not even to his enemies. In the area of domestic politics, whenever he has faced a serious challenge, King Hussein has known when to push, when to pause and when to make concessions. Beginning in September 1970, the Jordanian army crushed the Palestinian commando groups and over the next year expelled them from Jordan. Then, in March 1972, the king proposed a united Arab kingdom that would comprise two autonomous provinces, the East Bank and the West Bank of the Jordan river. In the 1970s, the Jordanian government cracked down on all forms of dissent, but in 1984, in response to demands for liberalization, the king convened parliament and gradually relaxed the ban on political activities. This culminated in the November 1989 multiparty elections after 22 years of suspended parliamentary life.

Algeria

Like Egypt and Jordan, Algeria and Tunisia are trying to transcend their authoritarian past partly in response to the changed global political environment but mainly in response to economic distress. Since it won its independence in 1962, Algeria has had one-man rule anchored by the military with a single legitimizing party, the National Liberation Front (FLN). It recently embarked on a process of democratization. The government of President Chadli Benjedid (1979–92) introduced a new liberal constitution, which was approved by referendum on February 23, 1989. By dropping all references to socialism and to the FLN as its vanguard, the new constitution represented a departure from the government's long tradition of building an Algerian identity on revolutionary foundations. The government also legalized political parties, and in June 1990 held local and regional elections.

At the time of these elections, President Benjedid was wrestling with two problems. The first was an economy crippled by the collapse of oil prices, which has cost Algeria $7 billion a year since 1986 and left 25 percent or more of the economically active population unemployed. The second concern was the emergence of an assertive fundamentalist opposition represented by the Islamic Salvation Front (FIS) under the leadership of Abbasi Madani and Ali Belhadj.

The FLN and Benjedid suffered an embarrassing defeat in the 1990 elections. In 1,541 local races, the FIS captured 853 seats while the ruling FLN won only 487. In most of the big cities, the FIS routed the president's party. It also won control of 32 of the 48 provincial councils.

Despite the FIS victory of June 1990, the FLN remained in control of the government, though its grip was tenous. President Benjedid, apparently convinced along with reform-minded allies that the Algerian political system would have to open up if it was going to survive, announced parliamentary elections for early 1991. He then postponed them until June.

The old order was not willing to go easily or quietly. The Algerian parliament, still an FLN preserve, passed a new electoral law on April 1, 1991, that illustrated that gerrymandering is a universal craft. Capitalizing on the FLN strength in rural districts, the new law constructed electoral districts that gave disproportionate weight to FLN strongholds. In the most egregious cases, one pro-FLN vote in rural areas equaled ten FIS votes in the cities. And runoff procedures were modified so that only the two top vote-winners would compete. The idea, it seems, was to preclude a third party occupying the middle ground between the FLN and the FIS.

In late May, the new electoral law sparked demonstrations that pitted the FIS against the army. The two leading figures in the FIS, Madani, who espoused political coexistence with other political parties, and Belhadj, a firebrand who was skeptical about pluralism, blasted the election law and urged their supporters to protest. The demonstrations prompted a declaration of martial law and the appointment of a new prime minister, Sid Ahmad Ghozali. Ghozali met with Madani in early June and committed his government to "free and clean elections" by year's end, but tension persisted. The army jailed hundreds of FIS members, and Madani and Belhadj were arrested for plotting against the government. The two leaders remain in custody, although most of their incarcerated followers have been released. The June elections were eventually rescheduled for December 26, 1991.

Following the uproar in May and June, the parliament could have liberalized the law. Instead it made it tougher. In the months preceding the December parliamentary elections there was a lot of speculation that FIS would be unable to sustain its popularity. Under the new constitutional provisions a group with as few as 15 members could register as a political party. But only a handful of parties had a serious following, and among them FIS proved to be far and away the most effective one on the hustings. With a turnout of over 60 percent of eligible voters and 49 political parties competing for their votes, FIS won the election in a landslide. It won outright 188 of 430 seats. Trailing far behind was the Socialist Forces Front with 20 seats, while the ruling FLN managed to win only 16 seats. The remaining seats were to have been decided in the runoff elections on January 16, 1992.

Algerian women voting in December 1991 in the first free parliamentary elections since their country achieved independence from France in 1962. Results gave the Islamic Salvation Front (FIS), whose goal is to create an Islamic state, a stunning victory.

The FIS victory sent shock waves through the Arab world, where regimes worried about the domestic effects of the looming ascendancy of the Islamic party. In the Arab press, opinion split roughly between those who applauded President Benjedid's commitment to the democratic process and feared that FIS would simply impose a new authoritarianism on Algeria and those who supported FIS. Within Algeria there was a similar split, and a significant segment of the urban population took to the streets to demonstrate for and against the FIS victory. In Algeria and abroad, many erstwhile enthusiasts of the electoral process changed their tune and argued that Algeria was not ready for democracy. One French politician, quoted in *Le Figaro,* a French daily, argued that it was foolish to expect "largely illiterate peoples to discover in just a few years what took us centuries to discover," while a Saudi commentator, Walid Abi-Mershed, noted that "The Algerian elections were another example of an attempt by a Third World society to adopt a democratic system which it is not ready, psychologically or practically, to accept."

In the days following their electoral victory, FIS officials professed to be willing to honor the precepts of democracy and took some steps to reassure wary Algerians. Algeria is no Iran. European influence—particularly French—runs deep in the former colony, where French is widely spoken. However, the democratic experiment came to a quick end. On January 11, President Benjedid resigned, apparently under pressure from hard-liners within the regime and the leadership of the army. Although the generals tried to give the new government a civilian facade, they had executed a coup d'état. In the Western capitals sighs of relief were more audible than condemnations of the coup. The January 16 runoff elections were cancelled, but the fate of FIS, which still possesses a residual legitimacy from its electoral triumph, is uncertain. Many observers speculated that the coup was more likely to postpone a transfer of power to popular forces than to prevent one. The FIS reacted to the coup with restraint and even dignity. There were hints that FIS might find common cause with its secular party rivals against the newly imposed government, which promises to rule until the presidential elections scheduled for 1993.

The stifling of the Islamists in Algeria has led some radical voices to charge the Algerian regime and its Western supporters with having double standards. If it is not possible to gain power lawfully within the system, then the only alternative—the argument goes—is to get rid of the system. Whether the Algerian army was right or wrong, justified or unjustified, there is no escaping the fact that its actions hardly bolstered the voices of moderation. In the weeks following the coup, thousands of FIS members were jailed, without charges, under the proclamation of a "state of siege." Shorn of their leadership, angry FIS members confronted the army, violently at times, causing many to worry that Algeria might collapse into chaos. All eyes in the Arab world were watching Algeria, the bellwether of a genuine opening. The outcome is not encouraging.

Tunisia

Like Algeria, Tunisia is caught in the throes of political liberalization, but unlike its neighbor, Tunisia has a more homogeneous political identity: there are fewer clan and ethnic cleavages and therefore its political system has been more stable. However, Tunisia's economy, like Algeria's, was rocked by the 1986 drop in the price of oil.

Save for a brief period of monarchic rule, Tunisia was governed by Habib Bourguiba and his Destourian Socialist party from independence on March 20, 1956, until Bourguiba's deposition on November 7, 1987. Until Bourguiba was ousted by then Prime Minister Ben Ali in November 1987, the government's legitimacy rested on Bourguiba's extraordinary personal leadership. He had played a prominent role in the nationalist struggle, he had a pragmatic ideology incorporating a pro-Western foreign policy, modernization and planned economic growth, and he dominated a broadly based political movement. Bourguiba consolidated his rule through the party and its patronage network, a bureaucracy controlled by the party, the provincial elite and the elite of his immediate constituency on the coast. By restricting allocations for military procurement, the civilian government was able to keep the military in check.

Bourguiba's regime was authoritarian and it grew increasingly so, particularly in the last decade of the "supreme combatant's" rule. The party was fused with the state, and the party bosses had a stranglehold on Tunisia's social and political life. This state of affairs, together with Bourguiba's heavy-handed treatment of the Islamists, prompted his removal.

Since he had no long-standing ties to the Destourian Socialist party and owed his presidency neither to an outright military coup nor to popular elections, Ben Ali sought to legitimize his regime by promising political pluralism and reform, an economic system that benefited the less-privileged, and the reactivation of the syndicalist movement to establish control over the economy.

Ben Ali instituted a multiparty system: he adopted a winner-takes-all electoral model similar to Algeria's in order to perpetuate the dominance of the Destourian Socialist party, which he renamed the Democratic Destourian Grouping (RCD) shortly after taking power; and he passed a law prohibiting the registration of overtly religious or regional movements. His objective was to preempt Rachid Ghanouchi's Renaissance party, whose earlier name was the Islamic Tendency Movement.

Ben Ali tried to incorporate the military establishment into Tunisian politics by promoting a number of military men to ministerial positions and giving them more influence than they had ever had before. Since he came from a military-security background, it is not improbable, as one observer noted, that the officers who supported his coup will coalesce into a junta to bolster his regime. Judging from Ben Ali's statements, he seems more inclined toward monarchic than pluralist politics. "The RCD is the party of the president and the party of change," he said. "We do not believe in a plethora of parties that will waste energy and create antagonism." Like his predecessor, Ben Ali may turn out to be a presidential monarch but without Bourguiba's charisma.

＊ ＊ ＊

In all these countries, a truly pluralistic political system can emerge only if power-sharing is institutionalized. A high level of civility, economic growth and a confident regime would also go a long way toward ensuring the survival of the democratization process, but these are precisely the qualities that are often absent. There are signs of severe stress in these societies. If participation is not channeled through stable institutions based on accepted principles, the incumbent elites may lose confidence and, in the name of law and order, reverse the process, as happened in Algeria. "If men are to remain civilized or to become so," wrote Alexis de Tocqueville, "the art of associating together must grow and improve in the same ratio in which the equality of conditions is increased." The "art of associating" will not be quickly mastered, and it would be unrealistic to expect overnight shifts from authoritarianism to democracy.

The country where political pluralism seems most likely to survive is Egypt, with its large educated class, its social and cultural unity, and a surviving memory of the constitutional period, which lasted nearly 30 years (from 1924 to 1952), a period when the opportunities for free political association and relatively free speech may have marked the high point of Arab democracy.

But in view of the prevalent sociopolitical conditions, the persistence of regional conflicts, and the lack of meaningful outside support for democratization, the opening of most of the Arab political systems is likely to be a slow, often painful, process.

New Political Alignments

One of the immediate regional repercussions of the Iraqi seizure of Kuwait was the emergence of new political alignments in the Arab world. In broad terms there was the anti-Saddam Hussein camp and those who were outside that camp. The former comprised the countries of the GCC, in addition to Egypt, Syria, Morocco and Lebanon. The latter included Jordan, Yemen, Sudan, Libya, Tunisia, Algeria, Mauritania and the PLO.

The members of the "anti" camp were divided into the oil group and the non-oil group. The oil group's attitude toward Iraq was exemplified by the GCC countries, who were afraid of losing their very existence—not to mention their way of life—at the hands of a powerful neighbor who they believed was ready to pounce. The immense military imbalance between themselves and Iraq reinforced their fear.

Well in advance of the January 15, 1991, UN deadline for Iraq's withdrawal from Kuwait, the Gulf Arab governments—particularly Saudi Arabia—had become so obsessed with their own security that they had virtually ruled out any dealings with Iraq. They insisted instead on war because an American-led attack would result in the destruction of Iraq and therefore ensure their security. The majority of the citizens of the Gulf countries seem to have shared the vision of their governments: the available evidence indicates there was no opposition of any consequence.

Beyond this, there was deep anger on the part of the Gulf governments at what was widely considered Saddam Hussein's treachery. The Iraqi president, these governments claimed, had made promises to King Fahd, President Mubarak and to the Kuwaitis themselves not to attack. Some even maintain that he had signed a nonaggression and mutual noninterference pact with Saudi Arabia on March 27, 1989, and a similar one with Bahrain on December 12 of the same year in order to mislead Saudi Arabia and the other Gulf countries. The agreements encouraged them to let their defenses lapse, thus enabling Saddam Hussein to deal with Kuwait without interference. In the tribal ethos, this is considered outright betrayal. Senior Arab diplomats from the Gulf region stress that a traitor deserves no forgiveness.

From the viewpoint of the non-oil Arab governments that joined the anti camp, Iraq's seizure of Kuwait raised the worrisome prospect that Iraq under Saddam Hussein might become a regional superstate. Despite the fact that members of this group shared a desire for financial rewards and a determination to contain Iraq, in key respects their agendas were quite different.

Egypt's Ambitions

Egypt appears to have had at least two additional reasons to oppose Iraq. The first was Egypt's ambition to recapture its preeminent role in inter-Arab politics. Saddam Hussein's fateful decision to seize Kuwait provided Egypt with the opportunity to do exactly that. "One can say that the power vacuum in the region…was the main factor behind Iraq's successful expansion into the Gulf area and its challenges of Western interests in the region," wrote Salah Basouny, former Egyptian ambassador.

Egypt played a central role in forging the Arab coalition against Iraq and insisted on the dispatch of Arab troops to defend the Gulf states. Bush's decision in the course of the Gulf crisis to relieve Egypt of a $6.7 billion debt to the United States was more than compensated for by the rock-solid Egyptian support for the U.S. position.

A second factor that helped shape Egypt's policy was Mubarak's desire to redraw the Arab political map by creating a new Arab alliance led by Egypt, Syria and Saudi Arabia, with Egypt hoping to act as a keystone of the security structure in the Gulf. This policy was based on the premise that the old Arab balance of power had crumbled and that the aftermath of the liberation of Kuwait could be chaotic if a new balance were not established. The fusion of Egyptian manpower with Saudi financial resources under an American military umbrella would have the advantage of counter-balancing Iran, neutralizing Syria's possible ambitions to impose its own design on the region, and marginalizing Iraq for a long time to come. In this case, a pro-Western Egypt could be a balancer, a keeper of stability and a beneficiary of the oil wealth of the Gulf Arab states.

Mubarak's Gulf policy was not all smooth sailing. Many Egyptians consider their president weak when it comes to domestic issues—the economy, democracy and stability—but an achiever with high marks in the area of foreign policy. In the Gulf crisis, Mubarak's policy looked vulnerable, and public opinion in Egypt was divided. The initial enthusiasm for Mubarak's anti-Iraq stand was dulled by the behavior of many Kuwaiti exiles, who sat out the war in luxurious Egyptian hotels; by the feeling on the part of many Egyptians that the Arab Gulf nations had not done much to help Egypt's ailing economy; and by shock at the intensity and volume of the allied aerial bombing of Iraq, where nearly a million Egyptians lived and worked.

The opposition was led by a coalition of parties, including the Socialist Labor party, the Muslim Brotherhood and the Communists. They called for an immediate halt to the "Crusader-Zionist onslaught of the Iraqi people," the withdrawal of Egyptian forces from Saudi Arabia and the linking of the Gulf crisis to the Palestine question.

In an attempt to appease the opposition and win public support, the Egyptian government stressed its commitment to justice and international legitimacy. It emphasized that once Kuwait was liberated, the allied forces should withdraw from the Gulf, and all the countries of the region, without exception, should destroy their weapons of mass destruction. Moreover, senior foreign-policy makers in Egypt, most notably Boutros Ghali (the UN secretary-general since January 1992), affirmed that if Iraq withdrew from Kuwait, Egypt would be able to coexist and cooperate with Saddam Hussein and that the allied partners were duty-bound to find a solution to the Palestinian-Israeli conflict.

Assad's Mixed Motives

The virulent personal animosity between President Assad and the Iraqi president played an important role in shaping the Syrian government's position. But power politics was also behind Assad's decision to join the anti-Saddam Hussein camp. Apart from the traditional Syrian-Iraqi conflict for dominance over the Arab East, other broadly related factors seem to have figured in Assad's calculations.

As early as April 1987 Gorbachev had warned Assad that "the reliance on military force has completely lost its credibility as a way of solving Middle East conflicts." This seems to have raised serious doubts in the Syrian leader's mind about the feasibility of matching Israel's awesome military arsenal. The subsequent Soviet disengagement from the Middle East apparently convinced him that, as a practical matter, the search for military parity was impossible in a unipolar world in which the United States, Israel's sponsor, was the preponderant power.

The logical alternative for Syria was diplomatic parity with Israel. For this reason, Assad may have decided that resuming ties with Egypt might strengthen Syria's hand in any negotiations over the conditions of peace with Israel. It might also smooth Syria's differences with the West and the Gulf Arab countries, thus broadening its options in the Arab East. Moreover, renewed ties with Egypt offered some promise of an American initiative to bring Israel to the negotiating table. This was probably the rationale behind Assad's visit to Egypt on July 14, 1990, a visit which ended more than 13 years of Egyptian-Syrian division over Egypt's separate peace with Israel. By lending Syria's support to the anti-Saddam Hussein alliance, Assad was sending a clear, if implicit, message to the United States: resolve the Kuwait crisis now, but be sure that the Golan Heights, West Bank and Gaza Strip are next on the agenda.

Assad's role was also influenced by his interest in Lebanon. For at least the past 15 years the Syrian leader's attention had been fixated on Lebanon, in part to promote pan-Syrian nationalism and reestablish a "Greater Syria," in part out of fear that hostile regimes, notably Israel and Iraq, would use Lebanon as a beachhead against Syria. Hampered by inter-Arab rivalries, the threat of an Israeli military thrust, and the discouragement of the superpowers, Assad could not effectively impose his will on Lebanon. With the Gulf crisis, however, the Syrian leader was able to make his move: he quietly swallowed East Beirut on October 13, 1990. In the process he ousted the anti-Syrian, Iraqi-supported, hard-line Christian leader, Gen. Michel Aoun. There was no significant opposition. The Bush Administration acquiesced in return for Syria's support for the U.S. Gulf effort.

A third consideration was Assad's desire to mobilize the Gulf states as a counterweight to Israel. In addition to obtaining their financial backing, Assad may have hoped to form a Syrian-led alliance composed of the smaller Gulf states, plus Iran and a weakened Iraq, possibly without Saddam Hussein.

Judging from past experience, Syria will probably continue to experience difficulty asserting itself in the Arab region. It is hard to imagine how Iraq's defeat will enable Syria to counterbalance Israel, especially since Egypt and the Gulf states have no strategic interest in encouraging the emergence of a hegemonic Syria.

Although Egyptians were divided, Assad had to contend with a public that was not at all sympathetic to his Gulf policy: a large majority of Syrian citizens opposed it. There were reports of sporadic demonstrations that the army summarily put down. For Syrians the issue was both political and moral. The birthplace of Arabism and a victim of Western colonialism, Syria had no business aligning itself with a Western-led effort to reverse Iraq's occupation of Kuwait when Israel for years had been occupying Lebanese, Syrian and Palestinian land with the help of American financing. The public also opposed the government's support of status-quo powers at a time when the old order was traumatizing every Arab society in political, economic and human-rights terms. But in a country tightly controlled by a heavy-handed regime, public dissent comes with a price tag. The city of Hama, which was leveled in February 1982 by the Syrian army in an effort to crush the Islamic opposition, stands as a chilling physical reminder of the cost of opposition.

The Syrian regime tried to put the best possible face on its position. After a stunning silence in the government-controlled media, the ruling Baath party claimed that it had hoped to save Iraq from its leader's folly. When that explanation failed to convince the skeptics, as was evident in the pro-Saddam Hussein graffiti and posters which appeared on walls in Damascus, Assad himself made a speech on September 12, 1990, to a group of parachute trainees.

He told them that Syrian troops had been sent to Saudi Arabia to accelerate the liberation of Kuwait. The sooner the Iraqi army withdrew from Kuwait, he maintained, the sooner the Saudis would ask Western troops to leave Arab soil. Assad implied that the Syrian troops would act like a UN peacekeeping force to prevent "Arab brother fighting Arab brother."

Another rhetorical attempt to placate domestic Iraq sympathizers was an official statement accusing the United States of using the Gulf crisis as a cover for "grand designs" against the Arab nation and warning explicitly that Syria might switch sides.

Two knowledgeable Syrian citizens who visited their country during the Gulf crisis and war told the authors that all the news was heavily censored, with very sketchy reporting on the war. Judging by the comments of senior Syrian officers and from Syrian newspaper reports and editorials, the Syrian government went out of its way to present the Gulf war as a Saddam Hussein-made reckless adventure, to state that Syria's purpose was to implement UN Security Council resolutions and save the victim from its victimizer, and to say that Syria would stand by Iraq "in the same trench" if it was attacked after its troops withdrew from Kuwait. The implication of all this was that Syria was acting on behalf of the interests of the Arab nation and in the name of international legitimacy.

The Dissenting Coalition

In Algeria and Tunisia, two members of the coalition who decided to stay outside the anti camp, pro-Saddam Hussein sympathies ran deep among the population. The governments, however, stayed more or less at arm's length from Iraq. The precise position of each of the coalition members may have been misunderstood because of the emotionalism surrounding the Gulf crisis and the coalition's rigid stance of "if you aren't with us, you're against us." Indeed, in the summer of 1991, Jordan published a White Paper explaining its position, which, it claimed, was distorted by those who disagreed. Second, most of the dissenting governments had started a process of political democratization some time before the onset of the crisis, and their position, at least in part, was shaped by the strong pro-Iraq sentiment of large segments of their populations. The pivotal questions, therefore, are: What was the dissenters' strategy and how, from their point of view, might the Iraqi occupation have been rolled back?

With regard to the second question, all members of this group opposed politically and as a matter of principle the Iraqi invasion of Kuwait. They also endorsed the Kuwaiti people's right to freedom and political independence. However, they seriously questioned the wisdom of condemning Iraq, arguing that such an approach would toughen Saddam Hussein's stance and make it extremely difficult for them to play a mediating role. They maintained that this was an inter-Arab problem and that the Iraqi president would not change his mind under threat. They opposed the deployment of foreign troops on Arab land, and claimed that if the crisis were left to the "Arab family," it would be resolved and the status quo ante restored. This contrasted sharply with the perception of the anti-Saddam Hussein coalition, especially Egypt and Saudi Arabia, who believed that because the Iraqi leader's main obsession was survival he would budge only when the "knife gets close to his throat."

Among the dissenters there were three groups, all of whom adopted similar positions but whose strategic objectives differed. The first were the Palestinians, and, contrary to the conventional wisdom, not all Palestinians sympathized with Saddam Hussein or even with Arafat. The second were the Jordanians. Jordan not only had a pro-Saddam Hussein population but its government had forged a strong alliance with Iraq long before the events of August 2. The third group consisted of Yemen and the Maghreb states. Yemen, the only Arab state represented on the UN Security Council, had to walk a fine line during the Gulf crisis, taking into account Arab-world sensitivities as well as the UN Charter. The Algerian and Tunisian governments condemned the Iraqi invasion but denounced the United States and its partners.

The Palestinians

Palestinians, even within the PLO itself which was portrayed to be avowedly pro-Saddam Hussein, were divided in their attitude toward the Gulf crisis. Arafat had embraced Saddam Hussein but without supporting his invasion of Kuwait. However, Arafat is not the PLO, and the PLO is not a monolithic organization. There were senior PLO officials who wanted the organization to distance itself from the Iraqi president on moral grounds: his invasion, they argued, violated the very essence of the Palestinian cause which opposes occupation. They also were against him on political grounds because the Palestinians stood to lose a lot by supporting a conqueror-dictator. Among these were the PLO's second in command, Salah Khalaf (Abu Iyyad), who was assassinated at the start of hostilities allegedly upon orders from Saddam Hussein, Khaled al-Hassan and his brother Hani, Jaweed Ya'qub Ghusain and a number of Palestinian intellectuals.

Many of the Palestinians living in Kuwait and elsewhere in the Gulf region saw the invasion as a disaster. Those who were wealthy or served in the higher echelons of the government bureaucracy strongly opposed Arafat's handling of the crisis. Many, including Fatah activists (the Fatah organization is a principal member of the PLO) in Kuwait, criticized the behavior of the Iraqis, and some even joined the Kuwaiti underground. Others, however, especially some of those who were on the lower end of the pay scale, were wooed by Saddam Hussein's pan-Arab pronouncements and his bravado statements on Israel. Of these, some believed that his annexation of Kuwait represented the first step toward the cherished goal of Arab unity.

Arafat did not condemn the Iraqi invasion of Kuwait but, at the same time, he supported the principle of Iraqi withdrawal. "The PLO took the position that while Iraq had violated a basic tenet of the Arab political order—the inviolability of state sovereignty," wrote Nasir Aruri, a Palestinian intellectual and member of the Palestine National Council, "Saudi Arabia and its Gulf allies in the GCC also challenged the institutionalized rules of conflict resolution within the 'Arab family' by acquiescing in U.S. military intervention." Arafat's position was supported by a number of leading Palestinian officials who appeared with Saddam Hussein on Iraqi television to express solidarity with Iraq in its stand against foreign powers but not in its conquest of Kuwait. The question therefore arises: Why did Arafat not condemn the Iraqi invasion, or, failing this, why did he not keep his distance from the Iraqi president?

On the first point, his desire to play a mediating role in order to find an "Arab solution," as well as his eagerness to accommodate the preferences of the Palestinians living in the occupied territories and in Jordan, weighed heavily in Arafat's calculations.

The second point poses a more subtle set of considerations. After the PLO's 1988 peace initiative had stalled and the efforts of Secretary of State James A. Baker 3d and President Mubarak to convince Israel to enter into negotiations with the Palestinians had failed, the PLO leadership in the summer of 1989 began to draw closer to Iraq. Arafat and his colleagues concluded incorrectly that the Iraqi military machine provided a shield against Israel.

The Bush Administration's suspension of the dialogue with the PLO in June 1990 pushed Arafat still closer to Saddam Hussein. The PLO found itself in the demeaning position of being forced to communicate with Washington through Egypt. For his part, the Iraqi leader was more than willing to play the role of a seductive suitor offering the PLO facilities, financial aid and the security of a "supergun." All this, it should be underscored, took place within a larger Arab context and a more specific Palestinian context. Until August 2, 1990, all Arab leaders, including Assad, expressed support for Saddam Hussein's attempt to close the gap between the Arab and Israeli military capabilities. On the other hand, the PLO's eviction from Lebanon as a result of the 1982 Israeli invasion and its subsequent confrontations with Syrian armor left the organization without territorial base or room for maneuver. If Arafat had had a secure place in Lebanon, or if his relationship with the Syrian leader had not been poisoned, his attitude toward Saddam Hussein might have been different. The fact that some of his close associates, including a few leading Palestinians in the occupied territories, entertained serious misgivings about the close relationship with Saddam Hussein and even about the Iraqi leader's deterrence bluff mattered little to Arafat.

To date, events have proved Arafat wrong. His greatest mistake was in not staying out of the crisis altogether and reaffirming the "nonlegitimacy of the acquisition of land by force and the unacceptability of resorting to military options in solving conflicts among states."

Jordan

The Iraqi invasion of Kuwait put Jordan's King Hussein in an unenviable position of aligning with Iraq and therefore jeopardizing the kingdom's economic relations with its wealthier Arab neighbors as well as its relatively privileged diplomatic ties with the United States. The king's most likely objective seems to have been to prevent foreign intervention and, failing that, to convince the United States and its allies to resolve the crisis through diplomacy. Sandwiched between Iraq and Israel, the two strongest powers in the region, Jordan felt well before the Gulf crisis that its very existence hung in the balance. The Israeli government's proposal that Jordan should become a Palestinian homeland and Iraq's threat to draw Israel into the war if Iraq was attacked gave rise to serious concerns in Jordan that it would become the main battlefield.

There were other pressures working on King Hussein. These included a pro-Iraq citizenry who had to be accommodated because of the democratization process under way in Jordan, and Jordan's dire need for Iraq as a deterrent to Israel. The Jordanian monarch had no illusions about a military solution to the Arab-Israeli conflict: Israel has decisively defeated the Arab armies on several occasions with conventional weapons, particularly its superior air force and its sophisticated military planning. What he apparently hoped to achieve by backing Iraq was an improvement in the Arab negotiating position in a peace process. This factor evidently contributed to King Hussein's feverish attempts to mediate between Iraq and its adversaries. In the process he traveled more than 50,000 miles and met with some 15 leaders, including President Bush.

Another major reason for King Hussein's decision to stay out of the anti-Saddam Hussein camp was his self-image: he is a descendant of a family, the Hashemites, that has played a major role in Arab history. The king perhaps hoped to turn his heritage to advantage at some future date when he and many other Jordanians anticipated more and more Arabs and Muslims would feel repelled by the intensity of the allied bombing of Iraq. He may also have hoped to woo the Palestinians, paving the way for negotiating on their behalf either single-handedly or jointly with the PLO.

Finally, King Hussein's antiwar posture coincided with his conclusion, after 38 years of alliance with the West, that the current Arab order had put the Arabs at a decided disadvantage vis-à-vis Israel and that a new order had to be created. The order he envisioned was based on a more favorable balance of power between Israel and the Arab states, and the Arab states' achievement of real political independence. By aligning itself so closely with the United States against Iraq, the Arab anti-Saddam Hussein coalition threatened to foil the emergence of such an order. The king may have reasoned that Saddam Hussein provided the West and Israel with the pretext for destroying Iraq's military power, leaving the Arabs more vulnerable than ever to Israel's military might. Therefore the Jordanian monarch did everything he could to prevent foreign intervention and the collapse of Iraq. After the war and the almost total destruction of Iraq, King Hussein had no alternative but to call on all parties to bury the past and forge an Arab reconciliation. The other members of the antiwar camp took a similar position.

The Maghreb States

Of all the Arab states that did not join the anti-Saddam Hussein coalition, the North Africans are the most interesting case because of their geographical distance from the conflict. Although they support the Palestinians and the Arab side, the conflict between Israel and its Arab adversaries did not shape their positions toward the Gulf crisis. As Mark Tessler, an expert on Maghreb politics, observed: "In all probability, Maghrebis view this dispute [the Gulf crisis] primarily as a symbol, or manifestation, of the weakness and misplaced priorities of Arab rulers. It is a reflection rather than a cause of what people judge to be wrong in the Arab world."

The Maghreb governments did not take a united stand, as was evident at their meeting in Algeria in September 1990. Morocco condemned the invasion and hesitantly sent 5,000 troops to Saudi Arabia. Tunisia, which condemned the Iraqi invasion as well as the deployment of foreign troops in the Gulf, was hoping, on the one hand, to play a mediating role and, on the other, to continue to host the Arab League headquarters. The Arab League headquarters had been moved from Cairo to Tunis as punishment for Egypt's signing a separate peace treaty with Israel in 1979. On September 10, 1990, the league decided to return the headquarters to Cairo, partly because Egypt was playing a leading role in the anti-Iraq alliance. Like Tunisia, Algeria and Libya disapproved of the invasion, but they also condemned the escalation of the Western military presence in the Gulf region.

Differences in their positions notwithstanding, the Maghreb governments lamented the failure of the Arab League to resolve the crisis, and made numerous attempts to find a peaceful solution. Senior diplomats from Algeria, Libya, Morocco and Tunisia shuttled back and forth between Baghdad and other Arab capitals with ideas and proposals, only to be rebuffed and sometimes even insulted. Saddam Hussein was unwilling to withdraw unconditionally from Kuwait, and the coalition aligned against him was not interested in an Arab solution—or in Saddam Hussein's withdrawal if Iraq's military power was left intact. Libyan leader Muammar al-

Qadhafi went as far as attempting to bring about a meeting between Saddam Hussein and King Fahd. King Hassan II of Morocco also tried to convene a mini-summit involving the main parties to the conflict to be followed by a pan-Arab summit. Their luck was no better than that of Jordan's King Hussein.

Fear of the political and economic consequences of a military confrontation for their own countries and for the Middle East in general motivated these governments. With the exception of Libya, all have serious economic problems, including high unemployment and severe shortages of foreign exchange.

The strong pro-Saddam Hussein, anti-Western bias of the North African people did not stem from admiration of Iraq's authoritarian ruler or his seizure of Kuwait but rather reflected anger at an economic and political status quo that benefited a privileged elite. In the 1980s there was a sharp downturn in North African economies and a marked increase in the number of people living in poverty. The growing gap between rich and poor, rising food prices, unemployment and a widespread belief that the system was based on patronage heightened public anger and led to a series of violent protests in Algeria, Morocco and Tunisia. One protest took place in Fez, Morocco, on December 14 and 15, 1990, when more than 100 people reportedly were killed in rioting. The government acknowledged 127 injured and 212 arrests. The targets of the protests were the symbols of privilege and authority, including five-star hotels and government buildings.

To the tens of thousands of people in the Maghreb who took to the streets to express their support for Saddam Hussein, he represented a challenge to the oppressive economic and political order. They saw the United States and its allies, on the other hand, as defenders of this order. The mood of the public, particularly in Algeria and Tunisia where political life was less constrained as a result of fledgling democratization, forced those in power to strike a balance between the demands of an angry public and the requirements of the state. Even in Morocco, which has not gone far in the liberalization process, King Hassan tried to accommodate the preferences of his subjects without alienating his traditional allies, the United States and its partners. He did so by his ill-fated mediation efforts and his declared commitment to an Arab diplomatic solution.

Windows of Opportunity

The Gulf crisis gave new urgency to finding ways to resolve conflicts in the Middle East. It also opened new windows of opportunity.

Iran is on the way to becoming again a respected member of the community of nations, after a tumultuous decade of attempts to export its unique variant of politicized Islam. Iran also exported a venomous anti-Western ideology that served to justify violent actions, including the taking of hostages in Lebanon. With the death of Khomeini in 1989 and the emergence of President Ali-Akbar Hashemi-Rafsanjani as the dominant political personality in Iran, there were indications—well before the Gulf crisis—that the revolution in Iran had run its course. The Gulf war marked the definitive end of the revolution. Iran unequivocally opposed Iraq's seizure of Kuwait and tolerated the allied action against Iraq while never condoning the permanent presence of foreign troops in the Gulf. Normalized relations between Iran and the United States are still some distance off. They were impossible as long as Western hostages continued to be held in Lebanon by pro-Iranian Shiites. But thanks to the tireless efforts of UN Secretary General Pérez de Cuéllar, by December 1991 all the hostages had been released, with the exception of two German relief workers who were being held by relatives of two Shiite extremists imprisoned in Germany.

Israel emerged from the war with enormous goodwill in the West. Although the Iraqi president tried to draw Israel into the war and thereby split the alliance, he failed. Israel sat through Iraqi Scud missile attacks without retaliating, making it much easier for the United States to sustain its alliance in the Gulf. More was at stake for Israel than simply forgoing the visceral satisfaction of revenge. In point of fact, there was little the Israeli military could have done against the Iraqis that was not already being done by the allies. Moreover, the Israeli leadership faces a giant challenge, namely accommodating the enormous influx of Soviet Jews, and it is counting on $10 billion in loan guarantees from Washington. By having been a team player, the Israeli leadership calculated that it stood a better chance of convincing Congress to approve the loan guarantee. However, continuing Israeli settlement in the occupied territories provoked President Bush to postpone a final decision on the guarantees until 1992, and it now seems unlikely that the United States will grant Israel more than a fraction of the $10 billion guarantee that it is seeking. In the process, Bush demonstrated that he was willing to stand up to one of Washington's most feared lobbies. Even more important, the public reaction to the President's decision was overwhelmingly positive and underlined a U.S. commitment to an evenhanded policy in the Middle East.

The Gulf crisis also cemented a new relationship between the United States and the Soviet Union. This is not to say that Moscow and Washington saw things exactly the same way—but then neither did the United States and France. When it came time to be counted, the former enemies found themselves on the same side. As a result, the UN Security Council has enjoyed an extraordinary rejuvenation. Many Third World nations also supported the alliance.

Changes at the UN

The former Soviet Union deserves significant credit for fostering the new mood of cooperation and activism at the UN. Throughout the course of the crisis, the Soviets voted in accordance with the Charter and against their erstwhile ally, Iraq. U.S. Ambassador to the UN Thomas R. Pickering has reflected frequently on the "shift in Soviet behavior" and its "greater willingness to condemn acts of aggression, even when perpetrated by a

Members of the Palestinian delegation arriving for the Middle East peace conference in Madrid (Oct. 30–Nov. 4, 1991) wave olive branches.

longtime friend, such as Iraq," as well as the striking cohesion of the five permanent members of the Security Council. Thus, when then Deputy Premier Hammadi visited Moscow in August 1990 to obtain a Soviet veto in the Security Council, which was debating enforcement measures for the UN-ordered embargo, he failed. Moscow voted with the alliance, as it did throughout the crisis. Moreover, when the Soviet Union had opportunities to scuttle U.S. diplomacy, as it might have done in the past, it did not exploit them. Rather than insisting on a public session of the Security Council to deal with the incident at the Al Aksa Mosque in October 1990 (when the Israeli police badly overreacted to Palestinian demonstrators and shot dead 19 of them), the U.S.S.R. agreed to private sessions.

The end of the cold war has been reflected very clearly in the Security Council, the UN body with the mandate to oversee the maintenance of international peace and security. A significant dividend of the recent dramatic improvement of relations between Moscow and Washington is that the Security Council has been functioning since mid-1987 as the collegial body anticipated in the UN Charter. Even cynical diplomats are speculating about collective security, a concept that appeared to have vanished along with the idealism of the postwar era.

Looking Ahead

Lingering disputes and old complaints are now resurfacing around the globe. The international response to the crisis in the Gulf demonstrated the potential for concerted action, yet one only needs to observe the disparate international responses to the bloody chaos in Somalia and Yugoslavia to note that not all breaches of the peace are treated equally under the new world order. The UN and the United States have been accused of using double standards. Many Arabs question the sincerity of the Security Council's commitment to enforce its resolutions in view of the numerous ones relevant to the Palestine question that are routinely ignored by Israel. They wonder whether the United States is as determined to implement UN resolutions in the Arab-Israeli case as it was in the Gulf crisis and war. Some senior American diplomats counter by arguing that widely accepted Security Council Resolution 242—the 1967 resolution setting the negotiating principle of giving up land in exchange for peace—was intended to be a framework for negotiations rather than a mandate for Israel to withdraw from occupied Arab lands.

There is widespread grumbling at the UN that the United States "hijacked" it and turned the world body into Washington's surrogate. Certainly, the United States performed throughout the crisis as the *primus inter pares*. One well-placed UN Secretariat veteran characterized U.S. diplomacy during the crisis as one of the most outstanding performances he had ever witnessed. Perhaps the key to the U.S. success was that it was a product of give-and-take. Retrospective assessments of the crisis are likely to persuade future U.S. diplomatic partners to insist on taking more and giving a little less.

Given the extent to which the United States achieved its goals during the crisis, some complaining is understandable. In fact, one result of the crisis is likely to be a concerted effort—in the next crisis—to circumscribe U.S. options, perhaps to the point of insisting that any forces deployed should be explicitly under the UN flag and command.

The UN will continue to be concerned with Iraq, and it is the strategy of Saddam Hussein's opponents to keep the world engaged. In addition, the UN will be challenged to prove its good faith in other areas. It is already being tested in Lebanon, where the government is pushing with surprising vitality and growing credibility for the application of UN Resolution 425 of March 19, 1978, which calls for the withdrawal of Israeli forces from the south and the restoration of governmental authority. The successful disarmament of the PLO in southern Lebanon in early July 1991 has undermined Israel's argument for the necessity of a "security zone."

Given the U.S. investment in blood and treasure to go to the aid of Kuwait, Washington might be able to influence the government of Kuwait to request UN monitoring of the October 1992 election. Doing so will not solve fundamental problems, such as limited suffrage or structural political defects. But international involvement in the election would move the Kuwaiti internal political debate to a different and more constructive level, as well as increase the chances that the voting is free and fair. Such a request by Kuwait would quiet U.S. public criticism of the government that the United States helped restore to power, while simultaneously signifying U.S. goals for the region as a whole.

There is unlikely to be a close analogue to the Iraq-Kuwait case in the future, but nevertheless there is now a somewhat greater chance that the UN, with the support of its key members, will live up to the promise of the UN Charter (Chapter I, Article 1) as agreed to by 166 states, including every state in the Middle East:

"To maintain international peace and security, and to that end: to take effective collective measures for the prevention and removal of threats to the peace, and for the suppression of acts of aggression or other breaches of the peace, and to bring about by peaceful means, and in conformity with the principles of justice and international law, adjustment or settlement of international disputes or situations which might lead to a breach of the peace."

Building on the Gulf Victory

We are trapped inside the text written by our rulers;
We are trapped inside religion as it is interpreted by our imam [prayer
  leader]...

—Nizar Qabbani, January 15, 1986

With all the finesse of an orangutan at a garden party, Saddam Hussein challenged the decorum and etiquette of Arab politics and exposed the divisions and tensions that divide Arab states from each other as well as Arab citizens from their governments. Though it was hardly his intention when he invaded Kuwait in August 1990, the Iraqi leader also succeeded in thrusting the United States into a position of unprecedented influence in the region.

The long-term effects of the 1990–91 events on Arab politics can still only be surmised, but the early evidence suggests that the impact may be profound. The crises of legitimacy facing many of the Arab regimes are no longer hidden from view by nationalistic rhetoric. The widespread disparities between rich and poor states, between wealthy rulers and impoverished citizens, are no longer camouflaged. The speed with which Iraq's army was defeated, as well as the necessity for Gulf Arabs to submit their fate to American soldiers, emphasized the impotence of several Arab regimes, despite the billions of dollars that they had spent on their war machines.

Most important, Arabs have not only developed a stronger awareness of their malaise, but they are coming to recognize the urgent need for change. Today many Arabs argue, without timidity, that the goal of their respective governments should be the promotion of the interests of their own people. They now realize and admit that Arab nationalism has been more the handmaiden of local political ambitions than a genuine quest for a pan-Arab order.

While the ideal that the Arabs constitute a single nation is still hallowed, the ideal provides a context rather than a motive force to Arab politics. The events of this fateful period have precipitated what will doubtless come to be seen as a new phase in Arab history, one that will be marked by transient alliances between regimes striving to promote their material interests while struggling to maintain their legitimacy domestically. No sooner had the war ended than cracks began to emerge in the Arab coalition that had united against Saddam Hussein. (The states that tilted in favor of Iraq had never formed an alliance.) The Arab Gulf governments preferred to put their security in the hands of the United States rather than risk inviting Syrian and Egyptian forces to establish a permanent presence in the area. From the perspective of the Gulf Arab leaders, it was safer to trust Washington than to trust Cairo or Damascus which might pursue political agendas uncongenial to them.

A new phenomenon in the Arab world is public opinion. People are demanding a voice in decisions that affect their lives, complaining about corruption in government and insisting that their leaders address their needs. Arab public opinion is far from monolithic, especially where opposition is tolerated. Even among Islamist groups there is a considerable diversity of views concerning the role of government and the definition of social justice and democracy. Where struggles for a freer political life are active, as in Egypt, Jordan and Algeria, there is a rich assortment of political opinions.

Arab leaders feel the pressure, as anyone who has been listening to them can attest. There is no conversion to Jeffersonian democracy, but many Arab politicians are responding to demands to open up the political system. They are pragmatic, and when they advocate widening political participation, they are not bent on political suicide, as was evidenced in the January 1992 coup d'état in Algeria. The Algerian army's move to stall the process of democratization illustrates the limit of political liberalization in the Arab world. These experiments in political freedom are bestowed, like a blessing *(minna),* only to be withdrawn when the ruler feels insecure. But this is an old game and few people are fooled by it anymore.

The most significant impact of the Gulf war may turn out to be, as one Arab scholar noted recently, that the "wall of fear" separating citizens from autocratic rulers has been breached. If a trend toward democratization is under way within the Arab societies—a task for years, not days—President Bush and the other allied leaders may have contributed to destabilizing the Arab world. The irony is that while the great powers applaud popular participation in government and exalt democracy, they fear instability; yet the achievement of greater participation and democratization without accompanying instability is difficult to imagine.

Peace Negotiations

On another level, the Gulf war opened up new possibilities for resolving the Israeli-Palestinian and the Arab-Israeli conflicts. In early November 1991, Israelis, Palestinians, Jordanians, Syrians and Lebanese met in Madrid and began what is likely to be a long process of U.S.-tutored negotiations. Secretary of State Baker confounded many skeptics by orchestrating that extraordinary moment in Middle East peacemaking. When the Gulf war ended, the Bush Administration was often criticized for its lack of vision and failure to come up with a peace plan to match the ambitiousness of its war planning. As 1991 ticked away, however, Washington had not only drawn up a broad peace plan but it was implementing it. The Madrid conference was followed, in December, by four parallel series of bilateral negotiations (between Israel on the one hand, and Syria, Jordan, Lebanon and the Palestinians on the other) in Washington. In January 1992, a conference to discuss regional issues, such as the environment, water and labor migration, convened in Moscow. Baker succeeded in persuading nearly all of the significant players to participate in the regional conference. The only important holdout was Syria, which argued that such a meeting was premature as long as the basic security and territorial disputes were not resolved.

The Arab-Israeli conflict has roiled the politics of the Middle East for nearly a half century, so the world can only hope that the present negotiations, under the aggressive prodding of the United States, will succeed. For years the Arab states were accused of being committed to the destruction of Israel. As Yehoshafat Harkabi, the Israeli academician and former head of military intelligence, notes, the Arab position has shifted fundamentally to the point where the Arab states are prepared to deal pragmatically with Israel. A significant sign of change was the 1982 Fahd plan, named after the then crown prince and now king of Saudi Arabia. A key element of the plan was a statement of principle that all states in the region have the right to live in peace and within secure borders. The problem is, as Harkabi notes in a recent unpublished paper, that while the Arabs have for the most part left behind their metaphysical commitment to Israel's destruction, Israel now has a government with a metaphysical commitment to keep the occupied territories. Thus the question now is, Will Israel be willing to reach an accommodation with the Palestinians and other Arabs that would mean giving up territories which it has occupied since the 1967 war, as well as security positions on the Golan Heights and in southern Lebanon? Whether the government of Prime Minister Yitzhak Shamir, who rejects the principle of trading peace for land, will prevail or whether a government more prone to compromise will replace it is the question of the hour.

Washington is counting on the negotiations to create their own momentum. Judging from the Palestinian delegation which attended the Madrid meeting as a part of Jordan's delegation but quickly acquired a separate identity, that may already be happening, and the results could reshape the Arab political landscape. After four years of rebellion against Israeli occupation, local Palestinian leaders are intent on grasping this last chance to free themselves. While the delegation of West Bank and Gaza Arabs cannot eclipse the PLO as the representative body recognized by the overwhelming majority of Palestinians everywhere, there is already a shift in the political equilibrium toward the Palestinians in the territories and away from Tunis-based PLO officials. Although Palestinians in the occupied territories deny it publicly, the texture and content of their relationship with Israel is changing for the better.

During the prenegotiation phase—following the Madrid conference and preceding the Washington phase of the negotiations in December 1991—the Syrian government of Assad, which has been implacably hostile to Israel, tried to rein in the Palestinian team and the Jordanian one as well. However, Syria lacks leverage in the post-Gulf-war period, and it no longer has a friend to lean on in Moscow. Therefore the shrewd Assad has little choice but to continue to talk, even if only to avoid isolating himself.

Though the chances for a peaceful negotiation of the Arab-Israeli conflict seem tenuous, they may never have been better. The governments of the region are hard-pressed to maintain the present levels of militarization and still meet increasing domestic demands. Arab phobias about Israel are receding. And the United States is demonstrating an impressive capacity for conducting sustained peacemaking. Moreover, though Israel has been able to count on massive transfers of aid and liberal loans from the United States in the past, there is strong domestic support for the Bush Administration's emphasis on ensuring that Israel's receipt of dollars from the U.S. Treasury should not undermine the peace process. All of this adds up to a propitious moment for peacemaking.

Although many commentators have written off the Middle East as immune to the tides of change gripping Europe, Asia and Africa, there is good reason to believe that these tides—the strivings for peace, democracy and prosperity—are also rising in the Middle East.

Talking It Over

A Note for Students and Discussion Groups

This issue of the HEADLINE SERIES, like its predecessors, is published for every serious reader, specialized or not, who takes an interest in the subject. Many of our readers will be in classrooms, seminars or community discussion groups. Particularly with them in mind, we present below some discussion questions—suggested as a starting point only—and references for further reading.

Discussion Questions

The political evolution of the Arab Middle East, as shaped by the turning points discussed by the authors, raises difficult questions. American observers should ask themselves why it is that the area is prone to such instability. Are there characteristics of its history which have made the above events inevitable? Are there reasons why the governments of the Arab Middle East tend toward authoritarianism?

Do you think that Western policymakers have been insensitive to the need to establish and support a vision for political freedom in the Middle East? Or rather have they given priority to short-term needs for dealing with various authoritarian governments?

Is it possible to transplant democracy as the Western world understands it to the Middle East? Why or why not?

READING LIST

Assiri, Abdul-Reda, *Kuwait's Foreign Policy: City-State in World Politics.* Boulder, Colo., Westview Press, 1990. Though this book was completed prior to the Iraqi invasion, it remains a valuable guide, especially to the domestic determinants of Kuwait's foreign policy.

Brown, L. Carl, "The Middle East: Patterns of Change 1947–1987." *The Middle East Journal,* Winter 1987. An authoritative study of the post-World War II era in the Middle East.

Freedman, Lawrence, "The Gulf War and the New World Order." *Survival,* May/June 1991. A reliable survey of the Gulf crisis.

Henderson, Simon, *Instant Empire: Saddam Hussein's Ambition for Iraq.* San Francisco, Calif., Mercury House, 1991. Although this book was completed prior to the Gulf war, it provides important background to the crisis. An appendix gives profiles of some of the leading members of the Baathist regime in Iraq.

Hermann, Richard K., "The Middle East and the New World Order: Rethinking U.S. Political Strategy after the Gulf War." *International Security,* Fall 1991. An incisive analysis of the Gulf crisis concludes with useful prescriptions for U.S. foreign policy.

Hourani, Albert, *A History of the Arab Peoples.* Cambridge, Mass., Harvard University Press, 1991. An elegant book by one of the leading historians of the Arab world. Strongly recommended.

Khalidi, Walid, "The Gulf Crisis: Origins and Consequences." *Journal of Palestine Studies,* Winter 1991. Examines the reasons for Arab support for Saddam Hussein.

al-Khalil, Samir, *The Republic of Fear: The Inside Story of Saddam's Iraq.* New York, Pantheon Books, 1990. Writing as Samir al-Khalil, Kanan Makiya provides a trenchant critique of Saddam Hussein's regime. Any careful reader will conclude this volume with a clear sense that the present regime in Iraq is deeply embedded and unlikely to be toppled even if Saddam Hussein disappears from the scene.

Kienle, Eberhard, *Ba'th versus Ba'th: The Conflict Between Syria and Iraq 1968–1989.* New York, St. Martin's Press, 1991. Detailed study of Syrian-Iraqi relations since 1968.

Legvold, Robert, "The Gulf Crisis and the Future of Gorbachev's Foreign Policy Revolution." *The Harriman Institute Forum,* October 1990. This brilliant analysis focuses on the Soviet reaction to the Gulf crisis and sheds light on the changed international environment.

Marr, Phebe, *The Modern History of Iraq.* Boulder, Colo., Westview Press, 1985. A lucid and dependable reference tracing the history of Iraq from the British mandate to the period of Baathist rule.

"The Middle East, 1992." *Current History,* January 1992. Entire issue. Annual assessment by experts includes articles on Israel, Kuwait, Lebanon, Egypt, the Palestinians and U.S. policy.

Muslih, Muhammad, *Toward Coexistence: An Analysis of the Resolutions of the Palestine National Council.* Washington, D.C., Institute for Palestine Studies, 1990. An analysis of the PLO's peace strategy through an examination of the resolutions of its governing council.

Norton, Augustus Richard, "Lebanon after Ta'if: Is the Civil War Over?" *The Middle East Journal,* Summer 1991. After more than a decade and a half of killing, the civil war in Lebanon now seems to have ended. This article explores the Ta'if accord of 1989 which ended the war, as well as the conditions under which Syria intervened in the fall of 1990 to begin the implementation of the accord.

————, "The Security Legacy of the 1980s in the Third World," *Third World Security in the Post-Cold-War Era,* eds., Thomas G. Weiss and Meryl A. Kessler. Boulder, Colo., Lynne Rienner Publishers, 1991. The challenges facing Middle East governments are those confronting Third World governments around the globe. This essay discusses the wide-ranging crises of legitimacy.

————, and Greenberg, Martin H., eds., *The International Relations of the Palestine Liberation Organization.* Carbondale, Southern Illinois University Press, 1989. A compendium of original essays dealing with the PLO's relations with the Arab states, the former Soviet Union, Iran, China and other countries, as well as a useful essay on the finances of the organization.

Rosenau, James N., *Turbulence in World Politics: A Theory of Change and Continuity.* Princeton, N.J., Princeton University Press,

1990. A compelling analysis of the global changes now tearing at the fibers of the international system.

Salinger, Pierre, and Laurent, Eric, *Secret Dossier: The Hidden Agenda behind the Gulf War.* Harmondsworth, Middlesex, England, Penguin, 1991. A combination of investigative reporting and diplomatic gossip detailing the Iraqi decision to invade Kuwait and the international reaction. In the first days of the crisis, a compromise settlement might have been possible, but the authors reveal how that settlement was allegedly undermined by Egypt, presumably under urging from Washington.

Seale, Patrick, *Asad: The Struggle for the Middle East.* Berkeley, University of California Press, 1989. A detailed and authoritative portrait of Hafez Assad by a veteran observer of Syria.

Viorst, Milton, "A Reporter at Large: The House of Hashem." *The New Yorker,* January 7, 1991. One of a series of articles on the Gulf crisis in *The New Yorker,* this focuses on Jordan and the diplomatic balancing act that King Hussein performed. See also Viorst's "Report from Baghdad," June 24, 1991.

Wohlstetter, Albert, and Hoffman, Fred, "The Bitter End: The Case for Re-Intervention in Iraq." *The New Republic,* April 29, 1991. Arguing that the war against Iraq was halted too soon, the authors urge the U.S. to finish the job by toppling Saddam Hussein. The article remains important for its examination of the moral and strategic implications of Washington's decision to fight a 100-hour war rather than to continue the battle.

Woodward, Bob, *The Commanders.* New York, Simon & Schuster, 1991. Although the Bush Administration has a penchant for secrecy, Woodward succeeded in penetrating the Administration to provide a lucid and informative account of the men behind the war. The book is particularly important for its portrait of George Bush as the main decisionmaker behind the war.